Family Favorites

FROM *ideals*

by Sophie Kay

CONTENTS

ABOUT THE AUTHOR

Sophie Kay is a vivacious, personable television personality and nationally recognized home economist. She was hostess-emcee of a daily cooking show on WGN-TV in Chicago and is currently doing a cooking segment on a television show on WISN-TV in Milwaukee. Throughout the country, Sophie has lectured and conducted many cooking schools for television, radio, newspapers, women's clubs, church and social groups, high schools and colleges. She appeals to cooking enthusiasts from all walks of life. Sophie Kay is a member of American Women in Radio and TV Broadcasting, American Home Economics Association, and is listed in *Who's Who of American Women.*

HELPFUL HINTS

ABBREVIATIONS

t.—teaspoon
T.—tablespoon
c.—cup
pkg.—package
pt.—pint
qt.—quart
oz.—ounce
lb.—pound

WEIGHTS & MEASURES

Dash .2 to 3 drops
3 t. .1 T. = ½ oz.
4 T. . . . . .¼ c.
8 T. . . . . .½ c.
12 T. . . . . .¾ c.
16 T. . . . . .1 c.
2 c. . . . . .1 pt.
4 c. . . . . .1 qt.
4 qts. . . . . .1 gallon
16 oz. . . . . .1 lb.

THIS FOR THAT
(Substitutions)

1 c. sifted cake flour . . . . .1 c. sifted all-purpose flour minus 2 T.
1 oz. unsweetened chocolate . . . . .3 T. cocoa plus 1 T. fat
1 T. cornstarch . . . . .2 T. flour
2 T. minced fresh dill . . . . .2 t. crushed dillweed
1 medium clove garlic . . . . .⅛ t. garlic powder
1 c. fresh whole milk .½ c. evaporated milk plus ½ c. water or
1 c. reconstituted nonfat dry milk plus 2 T. butter

SX517 BOOK VIEWER STAND — *The modern see-through book stand, made of strong, durable Lucite, completely protects cookbooks and other display items from smudges and dirt. The stand conveniently folds flat for easy storage or hanging. It's perfect for use in the kitchen, workshop, or home-study. A great gift idea and it's only $4.00, plus $1.00 postage and handling. Price subject to change without notice.*

IDEALS RECIPE CARD BOOKLETS—*Each booklet contains 32 individual 3" x 5" recipe cards, perforated for easy removal. Booklets are available in two distinctive designs and each includes a delicious easy-to-make recipe. Ideals Recipe Card Booklets may be purchased for one dollar from your local bookstore.*

Editorial Director, James Kuse
Managing Editor, Ralph Luedtke
Photographic Editor, Gerald Koser

ISBN 0-89542-614-5 250
COPYRIGHT © 1978 BY IDEALS PUBLISHING CORPORATION
MILWAUKEE, WIS. 53201
ALL RIGHTS RESERVED. PRINTED AND BOUND IN U.S.A.

Aloha Dip, p. 5

Appetizers & Relishes

MEXICALI RELISH
Prepare: 15 minutes
Chill: 1 hour

1 12-oz. can whole kernel corn, drained
¼ c. white vinegar
3 T. salad oil
¾ c. sliced pimiento-stuffed olives
½ t. celery seed

Mix together all ingredients. Stir until well combined. Cover tightly and refrigerate. May be stored for 2 weeks.

About 3 cups
Better if not frozen

TRIPLE CHEESE DIP
Prepare & Serve: 15 minutes

1 c. small curd cottage cheese with chives
1 3-oz. pkg. cream cheese, softened
1 4-oz. pkg. blue cheese, crumbled
¼ c. minced onion
¼ t. Worcestershire sauce
¼ t. seasoned salt
Dash tabasco sauce
8 small pimiento-stuffed olives, finely chopped
3 to 4 T. light cream

Mix together all ingredients except cream. Add enough cream to make dipping consistency; beat well.

About 2 cups
Cannot be frozen

OLIVE-BEAN RELISH
Prepare & Serve: 15 minutes

1 16-oz. can red kidney beans, drained
¾ c. coarsely chopped pimiento-stuffed olives
1 small onion, minced
¼ c. red wine vinegar
¼ c. vegetable oil
1½ t. sugar
¼ t. tabasco sauce

In medium bowl, thoroughly mix together all ingredients. Cover tightly and refrigerate. May be stored for 2 weeks.

About 3 cups
Better if not frozen

NEW ENGLAND RELISH
Prepare & Serve: 15 minutes

2 c. cooked small white onions
¾ c. halved pimiento-stuffed olives
¾ c. dairy sour cream
2 T. chopped parsley
¾ t. prepared horseradish

In medium bowl, combine all ingredients. Cover tightly and refrigerate. May be stored for 2 days.

About 3 cups
Better if not frozen

VERSATILE SPREAD
Prepare: 20 minutes
Chill: 1 hour

½ lb. Swiss cheese, coarsely shredded
1 T. minced chives
2 T. chopped green pepper
2 T. minced celery hearts
3 T. chopped stuffed olives
1 small tomato, finely chopped
½ c. salad dressing
¼ t. seasoned salt
Dash garlic powder
Few drops tabasco sauce

Mix together all ingredients; chill. Serve with party rye bread or assorted crackers. Also makes an ideal sandwich on your favorite bread, grilled or toasted.

About 3 cups
Cannot be frozen

SPECIAL APPLESAUCE
Cook & Serve: 45 minutes

2½ lbs. cooking apples
2 c. water
¾ c. sugar
1 T. aromatic bitters

Wash, pare, quarter and core apples. Add water; cook until nearly soft. Add sugar; cook a few minutes longer. Remove from heat. Add bitters; whip with wire whisk. Cool and serve.

About 2 quarts
Can be frozen

COCKTAIL FRANKS
Prepare: 15 minutes
Chill overnight

1 lb. cocktail franks or hot dogs, cut into ½-inch slices
2 green onions, sliced
⅓ c. wine vinegar
3 T. water
3 T. sugar
¼ t. seasoned salt
Dash tabasco sauce

Mix together all ingredients. Cover and chill in refrigerator overnight.

About 1 quart
Cannot be frozen

PEPPERCORN DIP
Prepare & Serve: 15 minutes

2 T. green peppercorns or 1 t. black pepper, 1 t. vinegar and ¼ t. salt
1 large clove garlic, crushed
⅓ c. Dijon mustard
1 egg
1 c. olive oil
Chopped parsley

Blend peppercorns, garlic and mustard in a blender until smooth. Add egg; blend until smooth. Gradually add oil by pouring in a thin stream and blending until smooth. Serve as a dip for breaded shrimp. Dip may be garnished with chopped parsley.

1½ cups
Can be frozen

FROZEN PICKLES
Prepare: 20 minutes
Chill: 2 hours

1 qt. unpeeled, sliced small cucumbers, about 1½ inches across
1 medium onion, sliced
2 T. salt
1½ c. sugar
½ c. vinegar

Mix together cucumbers and onion; sprinkle salt over both. Cover and refrigerate 2 hours. Pour off liquid, gently squeeze the slices. Do not rinse. Mix together sugar and vinegar. Pour over cucumbers and onions. Mix together lightly. Seal and freeze. Pickles may be refrigerated and eaten the next day or frozen for months.

1 quart pickles
Can be frozen

SPRING GARDEN DIP
Prepare: 15 minutes
Chill: 1 hour

½ c. small curd cottage cheese
1 T. finely grated carrot
2 t. freeze-dried chives
1 t. finely grated green pepper
½ t. seasoned salt
Dash garlic powder
⅛ t. dry mustard
Dash white pepper
1 c. plain yogurt

In small mixing bowl beat cottage cheese; blend in carrot, chives, green pepper, salt, garlic powder, mustard and pepper. Beat until fairly smooth. Fold in yogurt. Cover; chill. Use a dip for chips or assorted raw vegetables. Serve in hollowed-out center of a cabbage head.

About 1½ cups
Cannot be frozen

ALOHA DIP
Prepare: 30 minutes
Chill: 3 hours

12 macaroons, crushed in small pieces
¼ c. firmly packed light brown sugar
1 pt. dairy sour cream
1 large pineapple
Assorted berries
Seedless green grapes
Peaches, sliced

Mix together macaroons, sugar and sour cream. Chill several hours to soften macaroon crumbs. Do not stir again or macaroon crumbs will break into small pieces. Slice a cap-shaped piece off top of pineapple, about 1 inch below bottom of leaves. Hollow out center of pineapple with a sharp knife. Leave a firm shell to put the macaroon sauce into. Cut fruit into small pieces, discarding hard core that runs down the center. Fill pineapple shell with sauce. Replace pineapple top if you like. Place in center of large platter. Arrange pineapple chunks, assorted berries, grapes and peaches in groups around pineapple. If you like, sprinkle fruit with kirsch or brandy.

About 1 quart
Cannot be frozen

Bread

ABOUT BREADS

An easy way to tell when dough is "double in bulk" and ready for shaping: lightly press two fingertips about 1/2 inch into risen dough. If an indentation remains, bread is ready.

When dough has doubled in bulk, it should be punched down. Push your fist quickly into dough several times, pull edges of dough to the center and turn it over. Dough is now ready for shaping.

WHITE BREAD

Mix, Shape & Bake: 2 1/4 hours

5 1/2 to 6 c. all-purpose flour
2 pkgs. dry yeast
1 c. milk
1 c. water
2 T. sugar
2 T. oil
2 t. salt
Oil

Stir together 2 cups flour and yeast. Heat milk, water, sugar, 2 tablespoons oil and salt over low heat until warm, 120 to 130°. Add liquid ingredients to flour-yeast mixture; beat until smooth, about 3 minutes on high speed of electric mixer. Stir in additional flour to make a soft dough. Turn onto lightly floured board and knead until smooth and elastic, about 5 to 10 minutes. Cover dough with bowl or pan; let rest 20 minutes. For two loaves, divide dough in half and roll out into 7 x 14-inch rectangles; for one loaf, roll out to a single 8 x 16-inch rectangle. Roll from narrow side, pressing dough into roll at each turn. Press ends to seal and fold under loaf. Place in 2 greased 4 1/2 x 8 1/2-inch loaf pans or 1 greased 5 1/2 x 9 1/4-inch loaf pan; brush with oil. Let rise in warm place, 80 to 85°, until double in bulk, about 30 to 45 minutes. Bake in preheated 400° oven 35 to 40 minutes. Remove from pans immediately; brush with oil. Cool on wire rack.

2 1-pound loaves or
1 2-pound loaf
Can be frozen

7-IN-1 MINI-LOAVES

Mix, Shape & Bake: 2 1/4 hours

4 to 5 c. all-purpose flour
2 pkgs. dry yeast
3/4 c. milk
1 c. water
2 T. shortening
2 T. sugar
2 t. salt
1 egg
Melted butter (optional)

Measure 2 cups flour into large mixing bowl. Add yeast; blend. Mix together milk, water, shortening, sugar and salt in a small saucepan. Heat until warm (120° to 130°). Pour into flour-yeast mixture. Add egg. Beat at low speed 1/2 minute; scrape bowl constantly. Beat 3 more minutes at high speed. With a wooden spoon, gradually stir in enough flour to form a soft dough. Knead 5 to 10 minutes, until mixture is smooth. Cover dough. Let rest 20 minutes.

Divide dough into 4 equal parts. Shape into small loaves. Place in four 3 x 5 x 2-inch pans. Let rise in warm place until double in bulk, about 45 minutes. Bake 25 to 35 minutes in preheated 400° oven. Remove from pans; cool on racks. Brush with butter for soft crusts.

TRY ONE OF THESE VARIATIONS

CHEESE BREAD: Add 1 cup (4 oz.) shredded sharp cheese before the last part of the flour.

CORNMEAL BREAD: Add 1 cup cornmeal before the last part of the flour.

OATMEAL BREAD: Add 1 cup quick oatmeal and grated rind of 1 lemon before the last part of the flour.

RAISIN BREAD: Add 1 tsp. ginger and 1 cup washed raisins before the last part of the flour. Just before baking, brush tops of loaves with milk, then sprinkle with sugar.

RYE BREAD: Add 1 cup rye flour and 1 to 2 tsp. caraway seeds before the last part of the flour. Bake at 375° for the same amount of time.

WHOLE WHEAT BREAD: Add 1 cup whole wheat flour and grated rind of 1 orange before the last part of the flour.

4 mini-loaves or
2 small regular loaves
Can be frozen

Pictured opposite
White Bread

POCKET BREAD
Mix, Shape & Bake: 2 hours

5 to 6 c. all-purpose flour
2 pkgs. dry yeast
2 c. water
¼ c. oil
1 T. sugar
2 t. salt

Stir together 2 cups flour and yeast. Heat water, oil, sugar and salt over low heat until warm, 120° to 130°. Add liquid ingredients to flour-yeast mixture and beat until smooth, about 3 minutes. Stir in additional flour to make a moderately soft dough. Turn out onto lightly floured board; knead until smooth and elastic, about 5 to 10 minutes. Cover dough with bowl or pan; let rest 30 minutes. Roll into a 16-inch log, cut into 16 equal pieces and shape them into balls. Roll out to 5-inch circles. Place on greased baking sheets. Let rise in warm place 30 to 45 minutes or until puffy. Bake in preheated 400° oven on bottom rack about 10 minutes or until very lightly brown. Remove from baking sheet; immediately wrap in foil to cool. Cut pocket in bread. Pack wtih favorite filling.

16 pocket breads
Can be frozen

Cheese and Herb Bread

BAGELS
Mix, Shape & Bake: 3 hours

4½ to 5 c. all-purpose flour
3 T. sugar
1 T. salt
1 pkg. dry yeast
1½ c. water (120° - 130°)
1 egg white, beaten
1 T. cold water

In large mixer bowl, mix 1½ cups flour, sugar, salt and yeast. Gradually add water to dry ingredients and beat 2 minutes at medium speed of mixer, scraping bowl occasionally. Add ½ cup flour. Beat at high speed 2 minutes, scraping bowl occasionally. Stir in enough additional flour to make a soft dough. Turn out onto lightly floured board; knead until smooth and elastic, about 8 to 10 minutes. Place in ungreased bowl. Cover; let rise about 20 minutes. (Dough will not be double in bulk.) Punch dough down. Turn out onto lightly floured board. Roll dough into a rectangle, 12 x 10 inches. Cut dough into 12 equal strips, 1 x 10 inches each. Pinch ends of strips together to form circle. Place on ungreased baking sheets. Cover; let rise in warm place 20 minutes. (Dough will not be double in bulk.) Boil water (1¾ inches deep) in a large shallow pan. Lower heat; add a few bagels at a time. Simmer 7 minutes. Remove from water; place on towel to cool. Cool 5 minutes. Place on ungreased baking sheets. Bake in preheated 375° oven 10 minutes. Remove from oven. Brush with combined egg white and cold water. Return to oven; bake 20 minutes or until done. Remove from baking sheets; cool on wire racks.

1 dozen
Can be frozen

Pocket Bread

CHEESE AND HERB BREAD
Mix & Bake: 2 hours

TOPPING

8 oz. (2 c.) shredded cheddar or American cheese
⅓ c. minced onion
½ t. basil
½ t. oregano

Prepare topping ingedients but do not combine until ready to use.

DOUGH

1 c. warm water (110° to 115°)
1 pkg. dry yeast
1 egg
3 c. sifted all-purpose flour
2 T. sugar
1 t. salt
½ t. basil
½ t. oregano
3 T. soft shortening

Pour warm water into large mixing bowl. Add yeast, let stand a few minutes and stir to dissolve. Blend in egg. Measure, then blend flour, sugar, salt, herbs and shortening. Add ½ the flour mixture to yeast mixture. Start the mixer on medium speed or beat by hand. Beat until smooth, 1½ to 2 minutes. Stir in remaining flour with a spoon until flour disappears and batter is smooth, 1 to 1½ minutes. Scrape batter from sides of bowl. Cover bowl. Let rise in warm place until double in bulk, about 30 minutes.

Meanwhile, grease one 9 x 13 x 2-inch pan, one 11 x 7 x 1½-inch pan or two 8- or 9-inch square pans. Stir down batter in 20 to 25 strokes. Pour into pan. Now combine topping ingredients and spread evenly over batter. With greased fingers, make dents in dough, pressing almost to the bottom of the pan. Tap pan on the table. Let rise in a warm place for 20 to 30 minutes; dough should be no more than double in bulk. Bake in preheated 375° oven 30 to 35 minutes, or until golden brown on sides and top. Remove from pan; serve warm.

1 loaf
Can be frozen

NOTE: This bread may be made a day in advance and reheated in foil. Like all yeast breads, it freezes beautifully.

Swiss Wheat Bread

SWISS WHEAT BREAD
Mix & Bake: 1½ hours

2 c. whole wheat flour
¾ c. all-purpose flour
1 T. baking powder
1½ t. salt
1 t. baking soda
2 eggs, beaten
1½ c. milk
⅓ c. vegetable oil
¼ c. light brown sugar, firmly packed
1 T. instant onion flakes
1 c. (4 oz.) shredded Swiss cheese

Stir together flours, baking powder, salt and baking soda. Combine eggs, milk, oil, sugar and onion; stir in Swiss cheese. Add liquid ingredients all at once to flour mixture, stirring only until flour is moistened. Grease 4½ x 8½-inch pan. Line with waxed paper; grease again. Pour in dough. Bake in preheated 375° oven 60 to 70 minutes or until cake tester comes out clean. If necessary, cover last few minutes to prevent excessive browning. Cool in pan on wire rack 10 minutes before removing to cool completely.

1 loaf
Can be frozen

OLIVE CHEESE BREAD
Mix & Bake: 1½ hours

3 c. self-rising flour
3 T. sugar
3 eggs, beaten
¾ c. milk
3 T. olive oil
1½ c. (6 oz.) shredded cheddar cheese
½ c. chopped stuffed green olives

Stir together flour and sugar. Combine eggs, milk and olive oil; fold in cheese and olives. Add to flour mixture, stirring only until dry particles are moistened. Grease 8½ x 4½-inch loaf pan. Line with waxed paper; grease again. Pour in batter; bake in preheated 350° oven 1 to 1¼ hours. Cover with foil, if necessary, to prevent excessive browning. Let stand in pan for 10 minutes before removing. Cool completely before slicing. For extra cheesy flavor, serve toasted.

1 loaf
Can be frozen

GARLIC BUBBLE BREAD
Mix, Shape & Bake: 2 hours

2½ to 3 c. all-purpose flour
1 pkg. dry yeast
1 T. sugar
1 t. salt
½ c. milk
½ c. water
2 T. shortening
1 egg
¼ c. butter or margarine, melted
1½ t. paprika
½ t. garlic powder
1 T. sesame or poppy seeds

In large mixer bowl, combine 1½ cups flour, yeast, sugar and salt; mix well. In saucepan heat milk, water and shortening until warm (shortening does not need to melt); add to flour mixture. Add egg. Blend at low speed until moistened; beat 3 minutes at medium speed. By hand, gradually stir in remaining flour to make a soft dough. Knead on floured surface 25 to 30 strokes. Divide dough into 12 parts; shape into balls. Combine melted butter, paprika and garlic powder; mix well. Dip balls into butter mixture; place in greased 9 x 5-inch loaf pan, using 6 balls on each layer.

Sprinkle with seeds. Cover; let rise in warm place until double in bulk, about 45 minutes. Bake in preheated 375° oven 40 to 45 minutes or until golden brown. Remove from pan; serve warm.

1 loaf
Can be frozen

ITALIAN BREAD
Mix, Shape & Bake: 3 hours

6 to 6½ c. all-purpose flour
2 pkgs. dry yeast
2 c. water
2 T. sugar
2 T. vegetable oil
1 T. salt
Cornmeal
1 egg white
1 T. water

Stir together 2 cups flour and yeast. Heat water, sugar, oil and salt over low heat only until warm; stir to blend. Add 2 cups water to flour-yeast mixture and beat until smooth, about 2 minutes on medium speed of mixer or 300 strokes by hand. Add 2 cups flour and beat 1 minute on medium speed or 150 strokes by hand. Cover; let rise in a warm place until light and bubbly, about 45 minutes. Stir down. Add more flour to make a moderately stiff dough. Turn onto lightly floured board; knead until smooth and satiny, about 20 to 25 minutes. Shape into ball; place in lightly greased bowl. Twirl dough to grease all sides. Cover; let rise in warm place until double in bulk, about 1½ hours. Punch down. Divide dough into 3 equal parts; shape into balls. Cover; let rest 10 minutes. Roll each portion of dough into 12 x 8-inch rectangle. Starting at 12-inch side, roll up jelly roll fashion. Seal seam. With side of hand press ends to seal. Fold ends under loaf. Place on greased baking sheet; sprinkle with cornmeal. Using a sharp knife, make diagonal cuts about ⅛ inch deep across top of each loaf. Combine egg white and water; brush loaves with mixture. Let rise in warm place until double in bulk, about 45 minutes. Brush with egg white mixture again. Bake in preheated 425° oven 35 to 40 minutes or until golden brown.

3 loaves
Can be frozen

Pictured opposite
Cranberry Nut Bread, p. 12

SPREAD-A-BREAD
Mix & Bake: 1½ hours

2 c. all-purpose flour
2 T. sugar
1 T. baking powder
1 t. salt
2 eggs
⅔ c. milk
¼ c. vegetable oil
½ c. grated cheddar cheese
1 4-oz. can deviled ham
2 T. crunchy peanut butter
1 t. prepared mustard

Stir together flour, sugar, baking powder and salt. Beat eggs, milk and oil together; stir in cheese. Add all at once to flour mixture, stirring until just moistened. Spoon ½ of batter into greased 8½ x 4-inch pan. In small bowl, blend together ham, peanut butter and mustard. Mound filling lengthwise down center of batter. Spoon remaining batter around filling to cover top and sides. Bake in preheated 350° oven 1 hour. Cool 10 minutes. Remove from pan and cool on wire rack.

1 loaf
Can be frozen

Spread-A-Bread

CRANBERRY NUT BREAD
Mix & Bake: 1½ hours

1 egg
¾ c. sugar
1 c. dairy sour cream
2¼ c. all-purpose flour
1 t. baking powder
1 t. baking soda
1 t. salt
3 T. grated orange rind
½ c. chopped walnuts
1 c. cranberries, coarsely chopped

In large mixing bowl beat egg; add sugar and mix well. Carefully stir in sour cream. Sift together flour, baking powder, baking soda and salt; add to creamed mixture, stirring just until moistened. Add orange rind, nuts and cranberries. Turn into buttered 9 x 5 x 3-inch loaf pan. Bake in preheated 350° oven, 55 to 60 minutes. Let stand in pan 10 minutes. Invert and cool on wire rack.

1 loaf
Can be frozen

VARIETY SOUR CREAM PANCAKES
Mix & Serve: 30 minutes

2 c. all-purpose biscuit mix
1½ c. milk
1 egg
½ c. dairy sour cream
Butter
Syrup

In small mixing bowl at low speed mix together biscuit mix, milk, egg and sour cream. Using ¼ cup measure, pour batter onto buttered preheated 375° griddle. Bake until top is bubbly and edges baked. Turn and bake other side. Serve with butter and syrup.

VARIATIONS: After pouring batter onto griddle, sprinkle grated orange rind, chopped nuts, finely chopped apple, well-drained crushed pineapple, blueberries or thinly sliced banana on pancake. Bake as above. Serve topped with confectioners' sugar, a mixture of sugar and cinnamon or butter and syrup.

16 pancakes
Can be frozen

EGG BRAID
Mix, Shape & Bake: 2½ hours

4 to 4½ c. all-purpose flour
2 pkgs. dry yeast
2 T. sugar
2 t. salt
½ c. water
½ c. milk
2 T. shortening
3 eggs, slightly beaten (reserve
  1 T. for glaze)

In large mixing bowl, combine 2 cups flour, yeast, sugar and salt; mix well. In saucepan, heat water, milk and shortening until warm (shortening does not need to melt); add to flour mixture. Add eggs. Blend at low speed until moistened; beat 3 minutes at medium speed. By hand gradually stir in remaining flour to make a firm dough. Knead on floured board until smooth and elastic, about 5 minutes. Place in greased bowl, turning to grease top. Cover; let rise in warm place until double in bulk, about 1 hour. Punch down dough; divide into 3 equal parts. Roll each part on lightly floured board to make a 15-inch strand. On greased baking sheet, braid loosely. Pinch ends and tuck under to seal. Cover; let rise in warm place until double in bulk, about 30 minutes. Brush with reserved 1 tablespoon egg. Bake in preheated 400° oven 25 to 30 minutes or until golden brown. Cool.

1 large loaf
Can be frozen

Variety Sour Cream Pancakes

COLONIAL SALLY LUNN MUFFINS
Mix & Bake: 3 hours

1¼ c. milk
2 pkgs. dry yeast
2 t. sugar
2 eggs, well beaten
2 T. cream
¼ c. (½ stick) butter, melted
3⅓ c. flour
1 t. salt

In saucepan, scald milk. Pour into large mixing bowl; cool to lukewarm. Add yeast and sugar, stirring until yeast dissolves. Mix in eggs, cream and butter. Beat in flour and salt. Let dough rise until double in bulk, about 1½ hours. Fill well-greased muffin tins half full with dough. Let rise 1 hour. Bake in preheated 400° oven 15 minutes or until golden brown.

1 dozen
Can be frozen

CHEESY BEEF SNACK BREAD
Mix & Bake: 1 hour 10 minutes

3 c. all-purpose flour
1 pkg. dry yeast
2 T. sugar
1½ T. instant minced onion
1 t. salt
1 t. caraway seed
1 c. milk
¼ c. water
3 T. shortening
1 egg, separated
1 3-oz. pkg. corned beef, snipped
1½ c. (6 oz.) shredded cheddar cheese

In large mixing bowl, combine 2 cups flour, yeast, sugar, onion, salt and caraway seed; mix well. In saucepan, heat milk, water and shortening until warm (shortening does not need to melt); add to flour mixture. Add egg yolk. Blend at low speed until moistened; beat 3 minutes at medium speed. By hand, gradually stir in remaining flour to make a stiff batter. Spread evenly in greased 15 x 10-inch jelly roll pan. Brush with slightly beaten egg white. Sprinkle with beef and shredded cheese. Bake in preheated 375° oven 30 minutes or until golden brown. Serve warm.

15 snacks
Can be frozen

good - coarse bread ✓

QUICK CHEESE BUNDT LOAF
Mix & Bake: 2 hours, 15 minutes

FILLING

¼ c. (½ stick) butter or margarine, softened to room temperature
½ t. Italian seasoning
¼ t. garlic or onion powder
1 c. (4 oz.) shredded cheddar cheese

Combine butter and seasonings; mix well. Add cheese; mix and set aside.

DOUGH

 1 T. sesame seeds
2½ c. all-purpose flour
 2 T. sugar
 1 t. salt
 2 pkgs. dry yeast
 ½ c. milk
 ½ c. water
 ¼ c. (½ stick) butter or margarine
 1 egg

Generously grease 10-inch Bundt or tube pan; sprinkle with sesame seeds. Set aside. In large mixer bowl, combine 1½ cups flour, sugar, salt and dry yeast; mix well. In small saucepan, combine milk, water and butter; heat until warm (butter does not need to melt). Add warm milk mixture and egg to flour mixture. Blend at low speed until moistened; beat 3 minutes at medium speed. By hand, gradually add remaining flour, stirring to make a stiff batter. Spoon and spread half of batter into prepared pan; spread with Filling. Spoon and spread remaining batter over Filling. (If Filling is not completely covered, batter will rise to cover it.) Cover and let rise in warm place until double in bulk, about 1 hour. Bake in preheated 350° oven 35 to 40 minutes or until golden brown. Invert immediately; remove from pan.

1 loaf
Can be frozen

Quick Cheese Bundt Loaf

DARK PINEAPPLE DATE BREAD
Mix & Bake: 1¾ hours

 2 c. all-purpose flour
 ¼ c. light brown sugar, firmly packed
 1 T. baking powder
 1 t. salt
 1 8-oz. can crushed pineapple
1¼ c. (8 oz.) chopped, pitted dates
 1 c. chopped pecans
 2 eggs
 ⅔ c. milk
 ¼ c. vegetable oil

Stir together flour, sugar, baking powder and salt. In small saucepan combine pineapple with liquid and dates; cook over low heat, stirring until liquid is absorbed and mixture is dark and thick. Stir in nuts. Cool 10 minutes. Combine eggs, milk and oil; add date mixture. Stir until smooth. Add liquid ingredients to flour mixture, stirring only until flour is moistened. Grease 8½ x 4½-inch loaf pan. Line with waxed paper; grease paper. Pour in batter. Bake in preheated 350° oven 60 to 70 minutes. Cover the last 15 minutes of baking to prevent excessive browning. Cool in pan before removing.

1 loaf
Can be frozen

WHEAT GERM BREAD
Mix & Bake: 2½ hours

2¾ c. all-purpose flour
 2 pkgs. dry yeast
 ½ c. wheat germ
1½ t. salt
 1 c. warm water
 ¼ c. molasses
 2 T. shortening
 1 egg

In large mixer bowl, combine 1½ cups flour, yeast, wheat germ and salt; mix well. Add water, molasses, shortening and egg. Blend at low speed until moistened; beat 3 minutes at medium speed. By hand, gradually stir in remaining flour to make a stiff batter. Cover; let rise until double in bulk, about 1 hour. Stir down batter. Spoon into greased 9 x 5-inch loaf pan or 2-quart casserole. Cover; let rise in warm place until light, about 45 minutes. Bake in preheated 375° oven 35 to 40 minutes or until deep golden brown. Remove from pan; cool.

1 loaf
Can be frozen

*Pictured opposite
Variety Sour Cream Pancakes with Blueberries, p. 12*

WIENER BREAD
Mix & Bake: 1¾ hours

- 3½ c. all-purpose flour
- 2 T. sugar
- 1½ t. salt
- 1 T. shortening
- 1½ c. warm water (110° - 115°)
- 1 pkg. dry yeast
- 1 egg, room temperature
- ¾ lb. wieners or Polish sausage

Measure flour, sugar, salt and shortening into medium size bowl; blend. Set aside. Pour water into large mixer bowl; add yeast. Let stand 3 to 5 minutes; stir. Add egg and ½ the flour mixture. Beat 2 minutes with mixer on medium speed, or by hand until smooth. Add remaining ingredients and beat again with a spoon until smooth. Scrape down batter from sides of bowl. Cover. Let rise in warm place until double in bulk, about 30 minutes. Meanwhile, grease one 9 x 13-inch pan or two 9-inch round or square pans. Cut the wieners in half crosswise. (If sausage is over 1 inch in diameter, split lengthwise also.) Beat down raised batter in about 50 strokes. This is a thick, somewhat sticky batter. Turn into pan and push evenly into all corners with a spoon. Tap pan on table to settle batter. Press cut wieners down into the batter evenly so that there will be the same amount of bread around each piece, about 4 halves to a row, and 4 rows. Let rise as above until batter has doubled and starts puffing around the meat, 25 to 30 minutes. Bake in preheated 375° oven 25 to 35 minutes or until well browned. Remove from pan to rack. Brush with butter. Serve warm, cut into desired sections.

1 wiener loaf
Can be frozen

YOUR OWN BISCUIT MIX
Prepare: 25 minutes

- 10 c. all-purpose flour
- 1¼ c. nonfat dry milk powder
- ⅓ c. baking powder
- 4 t. salt
- 1½ c. shortening that does not require refrigeration

In large mixing bowl stir flour, dry milk powder, baking powder and salt together thoroughly. Cut shortening into dry ingredients till mixture resembles coarse cornmeal.

Store mix in a tightly covered container up to six weeks at room temperature. For longer storage, place mix in freezer containers and freeze.

To measure: spoon basic biscuit mix lightly into measuring cup; level with spatula.

15 cups mix
Can be frozen

BISCUITS
Mix & Bake: 20 minutes

- 2 c. Biscuit Mix
- ½ c. cold water

Using a fork, mix together biscuit mix and water to form a soft dough. Place on lightly floured pastry cloth and gently shape dough into a ball. Knead 5 times. Roll ½ inch thick. Cut into 10 or 12 biscuits, using a floured 2-inch cutter. Bake in preheated 425° oven 8 to 10 minutes.

10 to 12 biscuits
Can be frozen

NOTE: For drop biscuits, mix together biscuit mix and water to form a soft dough. Drop by spoonfuls (10) onto baking sheet. Bake in preheated 425° oven 8 to 10 minutes.

Wiener Bread

Soups & Sandwiches

LENTIL SOUP
Cook & Serve: 2½ hours

2 c. lentils
4 slices bacon, cut in 1-inch pieces
2 cloves garlic, minced
1 large onion, chopped
1 large carrot, diced
2 stalks celery, sliced
2 c. water
2 c. chicken or beef broth
2 T. snipped parsley
1 T. salt
½ t. freshly ground pepper
1 bay leaf
¼ t. thyme
1 28-oz. can whole tomatoes, cut in pieces

Place lentils in Dutch oven; cover with water. Heat to boiling. Boil uncovered 2 minutes. Remove from heat; cover. Let stand 1 hour. Fry bacon until limp; remove and drain. Add garlic, onion, carrot and celery to bacon drippings in skillet. Cook and stir over medium heat about 5 minutes or until celery is tender. Stir into lentils. Stir in bacon and remaining ingredients except tomatoes. Heat to boiling. Reduce heat; cover. Simmer 1 hour (soup will be thick). Stir in tomatoes with liquid. Simmer uncovered 15 minutes. Remove bay leaf before serving.

6 servings
Can be frozen

HOLIDAY SANDWICH LOAF
Prepare: 1¼ hours
Chill: About 3 hours

1 loaf (2 lbs.) unsliced sandwich bread, chilled (tinted if available)
Butter, softened

Remove crusts from bread. Cut into 4 slices lengthwise about ¾-inch thick. Spread 3 slices with butter. Top one slice with Ham Filling, spread second slice with Cheese Filling and third slice with Turkey Filling. Reassemble loaf, topping with plain fourth slice. Cover with a damp towel or foil; chill thoroughly. Frost about 1 hour before serving.

HAM FILLING

1 c. (7 oz.) ground cooked ham
⅓ c. dairy sour cream
¼ c. chopped walnuts
¼ c. pickle relish
¾ t. prepared horseradish
¼ t. basil leaves, crushed

In small mixing bowl combine ham, sour cream, walnuts, pickle relish, horseradish and basil leaves. Chill. Makes about 1½ cups.

CHEESE FILLING

1½ c. (6 oz.) shredded cheddar cheese, room temperature
¼ c. (½ stick) butter, room temperature
¼ c. dry sherry
½ t. salt
⅛ t. cayenne
Dash ground ginger

In small mixing bowl blend together cheese, butter, sherry, salt, cayenne and ginger. Chill. Makes about 1½ cups.

TURKEY FILLING

1 c. (7 oz.) chopped cooked turkey
1 8½-oz. can crushed pineapple, well drained
⅓ c. dairy sour cream
½ t. celery salt

In small bowl combine turkey, pineapple, sour cream and celery salt. Chill. Makes about 1½ cups.

FROSTING

2 8-oz. pkgs. cream cheese, room temperature
⅓ c. dairy sour cream
Radishes, thinly sliced (optional)
Green pepper, thinly sliced (optional)

In small mixing bowl beat cream cheese with sour cream until fluffy. Spread on sides and top of chilled sandwich loaf. Using cake decorator or serrated knife, swirl sides and top of loaf. Decorate top with flowers made from radish slices and green pepper slices. Chill.

24 servings
Cannot be frozen

HERB TOMATO SOUP
Cook & Serve: 20 minutes

Few sprigs parsley
½ t. basil leaves
1 t. celery seeds
¾ t. onion flakes
2 whole cloves
½ t. salt
Dash pepper
1½ c. water
1 10½-oz. can condensed cream of
tomato soup
Snipped parsley
Salted crackers

Make an herb bouquet by tying parsley sprigs, basil leaves, celery seeds, onion flakes and cloves in cheesecloth. Add to water with salt and pepper. Bring to boil; lower heat and simmer 10 minutes. Stir in soup; heat. Remove herb bouquet. Garnish with snipped parsley and serve with crackers.

2 cups
Can be frozen

MY FAVORITE HERO
Cook & Serve: 45 minutes

½ loaf Vienna bread
¼ c. (½ stick) butter, softened
2 T. prepared mustard
1 22-oz. jar baked beans
1 c. (4 oz.) shredded cheddar cheese
1 small onion, finely chopped
2 T. light brown sugar
6 frankfurters, split lengthwise
3 1-oz. slices cheddar cheese
Cucumber pickle slices

Cut bread in half lengthwise. With fingers scoop out bread crumbs leaving shell ¾-inch thick. Place bread on baking sheet. Combine butter and mustard; spread on cut surfaces of bread. In bowl combine beans, cheese, onion and sugar; spoon on bread, filling hollow and covering to edges. Place frankfurters diagonally on beans. Bake in preheated 350° oven, 25 minutes or until beans are bubbly and bread is warm. Cut cheese slices in half. Top each frankfurter with a slice of cheese. Place pickle slices on each cheese slice. Return to oven; bake until cheese starts to melt.

6 servings
Can be frozen

MINESTRONE
Cook & Serve: 1½ hours

½ lb. salt pork, diced
2 stalks celery, chopped
2 carrots, diced
2 large leeks, sliced thinly
1 Spanish onion, chopped
1 medium potato, chopped
1 c. string beans, chopped
1 c. shredded cabbage
1 c. frozen peas
3 medium tomatoes, peeled and diced
1 clove garlic, minced
½ c. brown rice
2 t. salt
¼ t. pepper
1 t. monosodium glutamate
½ t. thyme
½ t. marjoram
1½ qts. beef broth
Grated Parmesan cheese

Fry pork over low heat until lightly browned. Place vegetables, garlic, rice, pork and drippings in 4-quart saucepan. Add seasonings and broth. Bring to boil over low heat; cover. Simmer about 1 hour. Sprinkle Parmesan cheese over top before serving. Serve hot.

NOTE: In some parts of Italy elbow macaroni is used in place of the brown rice. To substitute, add 1 cup elbow macaroni to soup about 10 to 15 minutes before soup is done. Cook until macaroni is tender.

8 (1½ cup) servings
Can be frozen

My Favorite Hero

PASTA

For 1 generous serving, allow 2 ounces uncooked macaroni, spaghetti or noodles.

To keep pasta from boiling over, add a tablespoon of vegetable oil to the water.

If pasta is to be used in a salad, rinse it with cold water.

Sauces

BROWN SAUCE
Cook & Serve: 1¾ hours

4 T. butter
2 carrots, chopped
2 small onions, chopped
1 T. sugar (optional)
3 T. flour
3 c. Brown Stock
2 cloves garlic, minced
¼ c. coarsely chopped parsley
1 T. tomato paste
½ t. salt
8 peppercorns

Melt butter; sauté carrots and onions in butter about 30 minutes. Stir in sugar last 10 minutes, increasing the heat so vegetables will caramelize. (This gives the sauce a rich brown color; if you prefer to omit this step add a little Kitchen Bouquet at the end for color.) Stir in the flour and cook, stirring constantly, for about 4 minutes, or until flour is golden brown. Add stock, garlic, parsley, tomato paste, salt and peppercorns. Bring to a boil, stirring constantly. Reduce heat; cover and simmer 1 hour. Strain and serve.

3 cups
Can be frozen

QUICK BROWN SAUCE
Prepare & Serve: 20 minutes

1 clove garlic, minced (optional)
½ t. salt
4 T. fat
½ small onion, minced
½ small carrot, chopped
2 T. flour
2 c. Brown Stock

Crush garlic with salt. Heat fat; add vegetables and sauté until soft, about 5 minutes. Stir in flour and cook, stirring constantly, for 3 minutes or until flour is golden brown. Add stock and cook until thickened, stirring constantly. Strain and serve.

About 2 cups
Can be frozen

HOT RUBY CLING PEACH SAUCE
Cook & Serve: 20 minutes

1 1-lb. can cling peach slices
¼ c. catsup
2 t. lemon juice
2 T. sugar
1 T. cornstarch
¼ t. cinnamon
⅛ t. ground cloves
¼ t. salt

Drain peaches; reserve juice and combine with catsup and lemon juice. Mix sugar with remaining ingredients. Gradually add juice mixture. Cook, stirring, until thickened. Add peach slices and heat thoroughly.

2 cups
Can be frozen

LEMON SAUCE FOR VEGETABLES
Cook & Serve: 20 minutes

2 T. butter
1 T. all-purpose flour
2 t. sugar
½ t. salt
½ c. water
½ c. dairy sour cream
1 to 1½ T. lemon juice

Melt butter in 1-quart saucepan. Stir in flour, sugar and salt. Remove from heat; gradually add water. Cook over medium heat, stirring until thickened. Reduce heat to low; fold in sour cream. Add lemon juice and heat to serving temperature. Serve over hot, cooked spinach or broccoli.

1 cup
Cannot be frozen

BORDELAISE
Cook Bordelaise: 40 minutes
Cook Brown Sauce: 1¾ hours

1 c. dry red wine
2 green onions, minced
¼ t. tarragon
2 c. Brown Sauce
1 t. lemon juice

Place wine, onions and tarragon in small saucepan. Cook to reduce liquid to ½ cup. Add Brown Sauce; simmer 30 minutes. Strain; add 1 teaspoon lemon juice, salt and pepper if needed.

Serve with grilled meats.

2½ cups
Can be frozen

EASY HOLLANDAISE SAUCE
Cook & Serve: 40 minutes

½ c. butter
3 egg yolks
3 T. lemon juice
⅛ t. salt
Dash white pepper

Place butter, yolks and lemon juice in a small saucepan. Let stand at room temperature ½ hour or more. Five minutes before serving, mix thoroughly. Place over low heat. Cook, stirring constantly with wire whisk, until just thick, about 1 to 2 minutes. Stir in salt and pepper.

⅔ cup
Can be frozen

PAN OR BROWN GRAVY
Cook & Serve: 20 minutes

6 T. drippings
Pan juices
Brown Stock, water or milk
6 T. flour
1 t. seasoned salt
⅛ t. pepper
½ t. crushed marjoram
Dash Worcestershire sauce
¼ t. dry mustard

Skim off drippings in roasting pan, reserving 6 tablespoonfuls. Measure remaining pan juices and add enough brown stock, water or milk to measure 3 cups. Set aside. With wire whisk, stir flour, salt, pepper, marjoram, Worcestershire sauce and dry mustard into drippings in roasting pan. Stir constantly and cook over low heat until bubbly, thick and smooth. Add reserved liquid and cook, stirring constantly, until gravy thickens. If desired, twirl in 1 to 2 tablespoons butter and salt and pepper to taste.

3 cups
Can be frozen

LEMON BUTTER SAUCE
Cook & Serve: 10 minutes

¼ c. (½ stick) butter, melted
2 t. boiling water
¼ t. salt
Dash white pepper
1 T. lemon juice

Mix together all ingredients.

About ½ cup
Can be frozen

MUSHROOM SAUCE FOR GREEN VEGETABLES
Cook & Serve: 20 minutes

2 T. butter
1 c. sliced fresh mushrooms or 1 4-oz. can sliced mushrooms, drained
2 T. all-purpose flour
½ t. paprika
½ t. salt
½ c. milk
¼ t. Worcestershire sauce
½ c. dairy sour cream

Melt butter in 1-quart saucepan. Sauté mushrooms 3 minutes. Stir in flour, paprika and salt. Remove from heat; gradually stir in milk and Worcestershire sauce. Cook over medium heat, stirring until thickened. Cook 2 additional minutes. Fold in sour cream. Heat to serving temperature. Serve over hot, cooked green beans, spinach or broccoli.

1⅓ cups
Cannot be frozen

WHITE CREAM SAUCE (BECHAMEL)
Cook & Serve: 15 minutes

2 T. butter
2 T. flour
1 c. cold milk
½ t. salt
Dash white pepper
Pinch nutmeg (optional)

Melt butter over low heat; add flour. Cook and stir over low heat 3 to 5 minutes, until flour is cooked and sauce does not taste pasty. Slowly stir in milk; add seasonings. Cook and stir over low heat with wire whisk or wooden spoon until thick and smooth.

About 1 cup
Can be frozen

NOTE: A good white sauce for vegetables and fish. Use about ½ as much sauce for creamed dishes as for solids. Dilute with cream for a thinner sauce.

FOR CHEESE SAUCE: Stir in ½ teaspoon Worcestershire sauce and ½ cup grated cheese. Heat again over low heat until cheese melts.

FOR QUICK VELOUTÉ SAUCE: Use chicken, veal or fish stock in place of milk. Add 1 small onion shredded with 2 cloves garlic and ½ small bay leaf when adding seasonings.

TOMATO SAUCE
Prepare: 15 minutes
Cook: 1 hour

1 T. butter
3 T. olive oil
1 large onion, chopped
2 stalks celery with leaves, chopped
1 carrot, chopped
1 clove garlic, chopped
2 16-oz. cans tomatoes or 6 large fresh tomatoes
1 sprig parsley
1 t. salt
Dash freshly ground pepper
1 t. sugar

In large saucepan heat together butter and oil. Add onion, celery, carrot and garlic; sauté 3 minutes. Add tomatoes and remaining ingredients. Cook sauce gently, uncovered, until thick, about 1 hour. Strain. Store in refrigerator several days or freeze, if not to be used immediately.

FOR ITALIAN SAUCE: Add small bay leaf, 1 teaspoon oregano leaves, ½ teaspoon thyme and ¾ teaspoon sweet basil leaves, crushed. Simmer 10 minutes.

FOR MANHATTAN SAUCE: To equal parts of Tomato Sauce and Brown Sauce, add 2 cloves garlic, minced. Simmer 30 minutes. Slice 2 small onions thinly and sauté in 2 tablespoons olive oil or butter until transparent. Pour sauce over fish, grilled meat or roast poultry. Garnish sauce with sautéed onion slices. Sprinkle chopped parsley over top.

1 quart
Can be frozen

STEAK MARINADE
Prepare: 10 minutes

⅓ c. olive, peanut or vegetable oil
3 T. vinegar, lemon juice or white or red wine
1 clove garlic, cut in half
1 t. salt
⅛ t. pepper
1 bay leaf
1 onion, sliced

Combine ingredients. Pour over meat. Cover; chill all steaks 1 hour except flank. Chill flank 8 to 24 hours. Drain; broil.

About ¾ cup

BROWN SOUP STOCK
Prepare: 20 minutes
Cook: 5 hours

5 lbs. beef knuckle with meat
3 qts. cold water
1 medium onion, sliced
1 stick celery with leaves, diced
3 sprigs parsley
1 small bay leaf
¼ t. dried marjoram
10 whole black peppers
1 T. salt

Have knuckle cut in several pieces. Remove meat and cut in small pieces. Put half the meat in soup kettle; add water. Scrape marrow from bones and melt in skillet; add remaining meat; brown on all sides. Add browned meat and bones to soup kettle; cover tightly; simmer 3 hours. Add vegetables and seasonings; continue simmering 2 hours. Strain stock; chill.

TO CLARIFY: Remove all fat from stock. Beat 1 egg white until frothy; add to cold stock. Bring slowly to boil and boil gently, stirring constantly, for 5 minutes. Strain through several thicknesses of cheesecloth.

2 quarts
Can be frozen

BEARNAISE
Cook & Serve: 30 minutes

1 green onion, minced
3 crushed peppercorns
1 t. dried tarragon
1 sprig parsley, finely chopped
4 T. wine vinegar
2 T. white wine

Simmer all ingredients until liquid has been reduced to 1 to 2 tablespoons. Strain liquid into heavy, small saucepan. Proceed with Hollandaise Sauce recipe, omitting the tablespoon of cold water and 1½ tablespoons lemon juice. Cool the tablespoon of strained liquid before adding the yolks and starting the Hollandaise.

1 cup
Can be frozen

Pictured opposite
Mushroom Sauce for Green Vegetables, p. 21

Salads & Vegetables

GARDEN-FRESH SALAD
Prepare: 20 minutes
Chill: 2 hours

2 qts. boiling water
1 T. salt
1 7-oz. pkg. macaroni rings
1 10-oz. pkg. frozen mixed vegetables
1 c. diced cheddar cheese
1 c. mayonnaise or salad dressing
1 t. salt
1 t. onion salt
½ t. pepper
   Lettuce leaves

Bring water and salt to boil; add macaroni. Cook until tender yet firm, about 5 minutes. Rinse with cold water to cool; drain. Cook vegetables according to package directions; drain. Gently but thoroughly combine macaroni, vegetables, cheese, mayonnaise and seasonings. Chill. Serve on lettuce leaves.

6 servings
Cannot be frozen

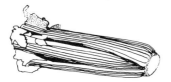

GODDESS CHICKEN SALAD
Prepare: 30 minutes
Chill: 2 hours

2 qts. water
1 T. salt
1 7-oz. pkg. shell macaroni
2 c. cubed cooked chicken
2 stalks celery, thinly sliced
½ c. Green Goddess dressing
5 radishes, thinly sliced
¼ c. sour cream
1 small red onion, sliced and separated into rings
1 2-oz. jar pimiento, drained and chopped
½ t. salt
½ t. pepper
6 slices bacon
6 medium tomatoes

Bring water and salt to boil; add macaroni. Cook until tender yet firm, 8 to 10 minutes. Rinse with cold water; drain. Combine macaroni with remaining ingredients except bacon and tomatoes. Chill thoroughly. Cook bacon until done, but not crisp. Roll up each slice with a fork to form a curl. Cut stem end out of tomatoes. Cut into eighths, cutting almost to, but not through, bottom. Gently open tomato "flowers"; fill with chilled macaroni mixture. Garnish with bacon curls.

6 servings
Cannot be frozen

FAMILY SALAD

6 c. mixed greens (Boston, butter or bibb lettuce, spinach, watercress)
   Tomato wedges
   Radishes
   Cucumber
   Carrots
   Hard-boiled egg wedges
   Croutons

Wash and dry greens; chill. Before serving, garnish with tomato and egg wedges, thinly sliced radishes and cucumber, grated carrot and croutons.

6 to 8 servings
Cannot be frozen

OVERNITE SAUERKRAUT SALAD
Prepare: 15 minutes
Chill: Overnight

1 26-oz. can sauerkraut, drained
1 large onion, chopped
1 green pepper, chopped
2 T. diced pimiento, drained
1 c. sugar
1½ T. caraway seed

Mix together all ingredients. Chill in refrigerator overnight.

8 servings
Cannot be frozen

POTATO SALAD SPANISH STYLE
Prepare: 30 minutes
Chill: 3 hours

2 qts. sliced cooked potatoes
1 c. sliced pimiento-stuffed olives
2 large stalks celery, chopped
1 green onion, sliced
½ t. salt
Dash pepper
⅓ c. French dressing
3 hard-cooked eggs, chopped
1 c. mayonnaise or salad dressing
Watercress

Combine potatoes, olives, celery, onion, salt, pepper and French dressing; toss lightly. Chill several hours. Add eggs and mayonnaise; mix lightly. Chill well before serving. Garnish with watercress.

12 servings
Cannot be frozen

SHRIMP POTATO SALAD

Cook and clean 1 pound medium shrimp. Coarsely chop all but 8 of the largest shrimp. Pour 2 tablespoons French dressing over whole and chopped shrimp; chill several hours. Add chopped shrimp to potato salad mixture in above recipe with eggs and mayonnaise. Serve garnished with watercress, whole shrimp and additional olives and hard-cooked egg slices, if desired.

6 main-dish servings
Cannot be frozen

CRANBERRY SALAD WITH MARSHMALLOW DRESSING
Prepare: 30 minutes
Chill: 4 hours

1 9-oz. can crushed pineapple
Water
1 3-oz. pkg. strawberry flavored gelatin
¾ c. sugar
2 t. lemon juice
1 large orange, ground
1 c. raw cranberries, ground
1 stalk celery, minced
½ c. walnuts, chopped
Lettuce cups

Drain pineapple; add enough water to syrup to make 1½ cups. Boil. Add to strawberry gelatin; stir to dissolve. Stir in sugar and lemon juice. Chill until thick as molasses. Fold in pineapple, orange, cranberries, celery and walnuts. Pour into oiled 8 x 8 x 2-inch pan. Chill until firm. Cut in squares. Serve on lettuce cups with Marshmallow Dressing.

MARSHMALLOW DRESSING

6 marshmallows, finely cut
1 c. dairy sour cream
1 T. lemon juice
¼ t. salt
2 T. sugar

Mix together all ingredients. Makes about 1½ cups.

9 servings
Cannot be frozen

STRAWBERRY-CHEESE MOLD
Prepare: 30 minutes
Chill: 4 hours

1 envelope unflavored gelatin
¼ c. cold water
1¾ c. boiling water
1 3-oz. pkg. strawberry flavored gelatin
2 T. lemon juice
2 10-oz. pkgs. frozen sliced strawberries, slightly thawed
½ t. red food coloring
2 3-oz. pkgs. cream cheese
Toasted almond halves

Sprinkle unflavored gelatin over cold water. Let stand 5 minutes to soften. Add boiling water to strawberry flavored gelatin. Stir to dissolve. Stir in unflavored gelatin, lemon juice and strawberries with juice. Stir until strawberries are completely thawed. Add food coloring to make a bright red color. Chill until thick as molasses. Pour about ⅓ mixture into oiled 5-cup ring mold. Form cheese into 24 balls, wrapping each around a toasted almond half. Place cheese balls gently on center top of gelatin being careful not to allow them to touch metal sides of mold. Spoon remaining gelatin on top. Chill to set.

8 servings
Cannot be frozen

GREEN BEAN SALAD

Prepare: 20 minutes
Chill: 3 hours

2 15½-oz. cans cut green beans, drained
2 medium carrots, sliced, cooked and chilled
1 large onion, thinly sliced in rings
1 large stalk celery, sliced
¼ c. cider vinegar
1 t. salt
½ t. sugar
⅛ t. pepper
⅛ t. dillweed
¼ c. vegetable oil
1 T. chopped pimiento
  Lettuce cups

Combine green beans, carrots, onion and celery. Mix together vinegar, salt, sugar, pepper and dillweed. Add oil; pour over vegetables. Chill 3 to 4 hours. Stir in pimiento before serving. Spoon into lettuce cups.

6 cups
Cannot be frozen

GOLDEN CROWN
FRUIT COCKTAIL SALAD

Prepare: 30 minutes
Chill: 7 hours

3 3-oz. pkgs. lemon flavored gelatin
2½ c. boiling water
1 12-oz. can ginger ale
1 c. dairy sour cream
1 20-oz. can fruit cocktail, drained
½ c. chopped pecans

Combine gelatin with boiling water; stir to dissolve. Stir in ginger ale. Gradually blend 3 cups hot gelatin mixture with sour cream. Chill both gelatin mixtures. When clear gelatin is partially set, fold in 1¼ cups drained fruit cocktail and pour into lightly oiled 1½-quart mold. Chill. When sour cream gelatin mixture is partially set, fold in chopped nuts and remaining fruit cocktail. Pour into mold on top of first layer. Chill until firm, about 6 hours.

12 servings
Cannot be frozen

PARTY PEAS

Cook & Serve: 20 minutes

2 slices bacon, cut in ½-inch pieces
1 stalk celery, sliced
2 green onions, sliced
1 c. finely shredded spinach or lettuce
1 t. flour
⅓ c. beef or chicken broth
1 16-oz. can peas, drained
½ t. seasoned salt
¼ c. toasted slivered almonds

In a 9-inch skillet, cook bacon over medium heat until almost crisp. Add celery and onions; cook until bacon is crisp. Add spinach or lettuce; cover and simmer 5 minutes. Stir in flour. Add broth; cook and stir until thick. Add peas, salt and almonds. Toss lightly, heating thoroughly.

6 servings
Cannot be frozen

STIR-FRIED BROCCOLI

Cook & Serve: 20 minutes

1 bunch broccoli
  (about 2 lbs., 5 to 6 c. cut up)
2 T. oil
1½ t. salt
1 t. sugar
1 T. beef broth or water
1 t. cornstarch
1 T. water

Wash broccoli. Drain. Cut the broccoli flowerets from the stem. Cut large ones into two pieces. Peel the stringy skin off the stem. Slice the stalk into 1½ x ½-inch pieces. Set aside. Heat wok or frying pan over high heat for 30 seconds. Add oil and swirl to coat the pan. Add broccoli and reduce heat to moderate. Stir-fry for 1 minute. Add salt and sugar and mix well. Add broth or water; cover pan. Cook 1 to 2 minutes. Stir once during this time. Broccoli should be tender but still crisp. Dissolve cornstarch in water. Stir slowly into pan. Stir and mix to coat broccoli. Turn off the heat. Serve hot.

6 to 8 servings
Cannot be frozen

Pictured opposite
Shrimp Potato Salad, p. 25

OLD-FASHIONED BAKED BEANS
Prepare & Bake: 7 hours

1 lb. (2 c.) dry navy beans
1½ qts. cold water
1½ t. salt
¼ c. brown sugar
1 t. salt
Few drops tabasco sauce
1 t. dry mustard
⅓ c. molasses
¼ lb. salt pork
1 large onion, sliced

Wash, pick over and discard imperfect beans. Add beans to cold water. Bring to boil; simmer 2 minutes. Remove from heat and cover. Soak 1 hour or more. Add 1½ teaspoons salt to beans and soaking water; cover; simmer till tender, about 1 hour. Drain, reserving liquid; measure 1¾ cups, adding water if needed. Combine sugar, salt, sauce, mustard and molasses. Cut salt pork in half; score one half, set aside. Thinly slice remainder. In 2-quart bean pot or casserole, alternate layers of beans, onion, sliced salt pork and sugar mixture. Repeat leayers. Pour reserved liquid over bean mixture. Top with scored salt pork. Cover; bake at 300° for 5 to 7 hours, adding more liquid if needed.

8 servings
Can be frozen

FILLED ZUCCHINI HALVES
Bake & Serve: 50 minutes

4 medium zucchini, about 6 inches long
1 c. water
½ t. salt
1 medium onion, minced
5 T. butter, melted
2 beef bouillon cubes
½ c. hot water
4 slices bread, toasted and cubed
2 eggs, beaten
¼ c. dry white wine or milk
1 c. (4 oz.) grated cheddar cheese
½ t. salt
Dash cayenne pepper
Dash nutmeg
Paprika

Place zucchini on rack in saucepan. Add 1 cup water and ½ teaspoon salt. Cover. Bring to boil. Reduce heat to simmer. Cook 10 to 15 minutes. Cut zucchini in half, lengthwise. Scoop out pulp; mash. Sauté onion in butter. Dissolve bouillon cube in hot water; add toast; mash. Combine with onion mixture and pulp; add all remaining ingredients except paprika. Heat until cheese melts. Spoon into zucchini shells; place in shallow baking dish. Sprinkle with paprika. Bake in preheated 350° oven, 15 to 20 minutes.

8 servings
Can be frozen

BAVARIAN WAX BEANS
Cook & Serve: 15 minutes

4 slices bacon, cut in ½-inch pieces
2 green onions, sliced
1 stalk celery, diagonally sliced
1 16-oz. can beans, drained
⅓ c. white wine vinegar
¾ t. salt
3 T. sugar
1 T. diced pimiento, drained

In 9-inch skillet, cook bacon over medium heat until almost crisp. Drain off bacon drippings, leaving 2 tablespoons in the skillet. Add onions and celery; stir-fry until bacon is crisp. Stir in beans, vinegar, salt and sugar; heat thoroughly. Top with pimiento.

4 servings
Can be frozen

CRUNCHY GREEN BEANS
Cook & Serve: 15 minutes

¼ c. (½ stick) butter or margarine
¼ c. chopped salted peanuts
¼ t. salt
Dash fresh ground pepper
Dash nutmeg
1 T. lemon juice
1 16-oz. can whole, cut or French style green beans

Melt butter; add peanuts. Sauté until golden brown. Add seasonings and lemon juice. Heat beans; drain; pour peanut mixture over beans.

3 to 4 servings
Can be frozen

NOTE: This recipe may also be used with lima beans, peas, etc.

OVEN-ROASTED POTATOES
Bake & Serve: 1 hour

8 medium potatoes, pared
½ c. (1 stick) butter
1 small onion, minced
Salt
Pepper

Cut potatoes into quarters. Cook in boiling salted water 15 minutes. Melt butter in small saucepan. Add onion and sauté until golden brown. Drain potatoes. Place in shallow pan (bottom half of broiler or jelly roll pan). Pour half of onion-butter mixture over all. Bake in preheated 400° oven about 15 minutes; turn and coat with remaining onion-butter mixture. Serve when tender and crisp golden brown. Season with salt and pepper.

8 servings
Can be frozen

ZUCCHINI-ITALIAN STYLE
Cook & Serve: 25 minutes

2 T. olive oil
2 small onions, sliced
1 lb. small zucchini, 1½-inches in diameter, washed
1 t. seasoned salt
¼ t. pepper
2 t. sweet basil, crushed
3 medium tomatoes, peeled and sliced

Heat oil in large skillet. Add onions. Sauté 3 minutes or until golden brown. Cut zucchini in ¼-inch slices. Add with remaining ingredients to onions. Cover; simmer 8 minutes. Uncover and simmer 5 minutes or until barely tender.

4 to 6 servings
Cannot be frozen

POTATO CLOUDS
Mix & Bake: 1 hour 15 minutes

2 c. (4 servings) prepared instant mashed potatoes
1 c. cottage cheese
½ c. dairy sour cream
¼ c. minced onion
Salt
Dash white pepper
1 t. minced parsley
¼ t. garlic salt
3 egg yolks, slightly beaten
3 egg whites, stiffly beaten

Prepare instant mashed potatoes as directed on package, omitting milk and butter. Add remaining ingredients except egg whites. Fold in egg whites; pour into 2-quart casserole or eight 6-ounce custard cups. Bake in preheated 350° oven 1 hour for casserole, 40 to 45 minutes for custard cups.

8 servings
Cannot be frozen

PEANUT-STUFFED SQUASH
Prepare & Serve: 1½ hours

2 acorn squash
2 T. butter
¾ lb. (2 c.) minced baked ham
2 T. minced onion
1 T. firmly packed light brown sugar
1 T. grated orange rind
¼ c. orange juice
1 t. salt
1 c. peanuts, chopped
1½ T. melted butter
¼ c. chopped parsley

Halve squash and remove seeds. Place squash, cut side down, on greased baking sheet. Bake in preheated 350° oven 45 minutes or until tender. Scoop pulp out of squash into a mixing bowl leaving a thin shell. In a small skillet melt 2 tablespoons butter and lightly brown ham and onion. Stir into squash; add brown sugar, orange rind, juice, salt and peanuts. Refill shells with mixture; drizzle with melted butter. Bake in preheated 350° oven 20 to 30 minutes, until heated through. Garnish with chopped parsley.

4 servings
Can be frozen

SCALLOPED TOMATOES
Bake & Serve: 30 minutes

1½ c. torn bread
¼ c. (½ stick) butter, melted
2½ c. (1 20-oz. can) tomatoes.
1 T. brown sugar
¼ t. sweet basil
½ t. salt
1 small onion, chopped
1 small stalk celery, chopped

Place bread in the bottom of a shallow 1½-quart baking dish. Pour melted butter over bread. Add remaining ingredients. Stir gently to combine well. Bake in preheated 400° oven 20 minutes.

8 servings
Can be frozen

Main Dishes

BEEF

```
GUIDELINES FOR BUYING MEAT
          (per serving)

Uncooked bone-in meat: allow ½ to
   ¾ pound
Uncooked boneless meat: allow
   ⅓ pound

Cooked bone-in meat: allow ⅓ pound
Cooked boneless meat: allow ⅛ to
   ¼ pound
```

HARVEST ROUND STEAK
Cook & Serve: 2½ hours

2½ lbs. beef round steak, cut ¾ to 1 inch
    thick
  3 T. flour
  1 t. salt
 ⅛ t. pepper
  3 T. vegetable oil or cooking fat
  1 cinnamon stick
  3 small onions, cut in half
  6 small fresh yams (about 1½ lbs.), pared
 ½ c. water
  2 medium tart red cooking apples,
    cored and quartered
    Sugar, if desired
    Water
  2 T. flour
 ¼ t. salt

Cut round steak into 6 portions. Combine 3 tablespoons flour, 1 teaspoon salt and pepper. Dredge meat in seasoned flour. Heat fat in Dutch oven. Add meat and brown on both sides. Pour off drippings. Add cinnamon stick, onions, yams and ½ cup water. Cover tightly; bake in 325° oven 2 hours. Remove onions and cinnamon stick. Add apples, cover and bake 15 to 20 minutes or until meat and apples are done. Remove meat, yams and apples to warm serving platter. Sprinkle apples with sugar, if desired. Measure cook-

ing liquid and add water to make 1½ cups. Blend 2 tablespoons flour with ½ cup additional water. Add to cooking liquid. Cook, stirring until thickened. Season with ¼ teaspoon salt. Serve gravy with meat, yams and apples.

6 servings
Can be frozen

BEEF TIP ROAST
Roast: 30 to 40 minutes per pound

3½- to 8-lb. beef tip roast

Place roast, fat side up, on rack in open roasting pan. Insert meat thermometer so bulb is centered in the thickest part. Do not cover or add water. Roast in a 325° oven to desired degree of doneness: 140° for rare; 160° for medium; 170° for well done. For a 3½- to 5-pound roast, allow 35 to 40 minutes per pound. For a 6- to 8-pound roast, allow 30 to 35 minutes per pound. For easier carving, let roast "stand" in a warm place 15 to 20 minutes after removing from oven. Since roast usually continues to cook after it is removed from oven, it is best to remove it about 5° below temperature desired.

Allow ⅛ to ¼ pound per serving
Can be frozen

DOUBLE-PEACHY CORNED BEEF OVEN ROAST
Roast & Serve: 3 hours

    Corned beef for oven roasting
  1 c. peach preserves
  1 T. lemon juice
 ¼ t. ginger

Place roast, fat side up, on rack in shallow roasting pan. Roast in 325° oven until fork tender, 2¼ to 2¾ hours. If a sharp-tined meat fork can be inserted and removed easily, the meat is fork tender. Combine peach preserves, lemon juice and ginger. During the last half hour of roasting time, spoon glaze over corned beef. Let stand 15 minutes before slicing.

Allow ½ pound per serving
Can be frozen

Pictured opposite
Bountiful Beef Stew, p. 32

PLANKED BEEF FIESTA PATTIES
Broil & Serve: 45 minutes

- 2 lbs. ground chuck
- 2 t. salt
- ¼ t. pepper
- ¼ c. catsup
- ¼ c. shredded cheddar cheese
- 2 T. chopped green pepper
- 2 c. seasoned mashed potatoes
- 2 T. melted butter

Combine beef with salt and pepper; shape into 6 to 8 patties, ½ to ¾ inch thick. Place patties on rack under broiler 2 to 3 inches from heat. Broil 8 to 10 minutes on one side. Turn; broil 5 to 10 minutes longer, until done to taste. Remove patties from broiler. Top each with catsup, cheese and green pepper. Transfer patties to warm sizzle platter or oiled wooden plank. Tube or spoon mashed potatoes around patties. Brush with melted butter. Return to broiler until potatoes are lightly browned and cheese is melted, about 3 minutes.

6 to 8 servings
Can be frozen

BOUNTIFUL BEEF STEW
Cook & Serve: 3½ hours

- ¼ c flour
- 2 t. salt
- ¼ t. pepper
- 2 lbs. boneless beef for stew
- 3 T. drippings or vegetable oil
- 2 c. water
- ½ t. basil
- ¼ t. marjoram
- 2 medium onions, sliced
- 1 10-oz. pkg. frozen Brussels sprouts
- 1 23-oz. can sweet potatoes, drained and cut in pieces
  Flour for gravy, if desired

Combine ¼ cup flour, salt and pepper. Dredge meat in seasoned flour. Heat drippings to 350°. Brown beef. Pour off drippings. Add water, basil, marjoram and onions. Cover tightly; cook slowly 2½ hours. Add Brussels sprouts; cook 15 minutes. Add sweet potatoes; cook 15 minutes longer or until meat is tender and vegetables are done. Remove meat and vegetables to warm serving platter. Thicken cooking liquid with flour for gravy, if desired.

6 to 8 servings
Can be frozen

Olé Cheeseburger Pie

OLÉ CHEESEBURGER PIE
Prepare & Serve: 1 hour

- ¼ c. olive oil
- 1 lb. frozen Southern-style hash brown potatoes
- ½ t. salt
- ½ t. crushed oregano
- ⅛ t. pepper
- 1 c. (4 oz.) shredded cheddar cheese
- 1 egg, slightly beaten
- 1 T. olive oil
- 1 small onion, chopped
- ½ green pepper, chopped
- 1 lb. ground chuck
- 1 T. flour
- 1 T. water
- 1 8-oz. can tomato sauce
- ½ t. seasoned salt
  Dash pepper
- 1 whole pimiento, cut in strips
- 2 slices cooked bacon, crumbled

Heat ¼ cup oil in large skillet; add potatoes. Cook, stirring occasionally, until tender and lightly browned. Remove from heat. Stir in salt, oregano, pepper and ¼ cup cheese. Cool about 3 minutes. Stir in egg. Press mixture into 9-inch pie pan to form a shell. Bake in preheated 400° oven 15 minutes. Meanwhile, heat 1 tablespoon olive oil in skillet; add onion and green pepper; cook until onion is golden brown. Stir in beef; cook until browned. Mix flour and water; add to meat with tomato sauce, seasoned salt and pepper. Cook and stir until thickened. Fill hot potato shell with meat mixture. Sprinkle remaining cheese over top. Arrange pimiento strips on top and sprinkle bacon bits over all. Return to oven until cheese melts, about 2 minutes. Remove from oven; let stand 2 to 3 minutes. Cut in wedges and serve.

6 servings
Can be frozen

PATCHWORK CASSEROLE
Prepare & Serve: 1½ hours

2 lbs. ground chuck
2 green peppers, chopped
1 large onion, chopped
2 lbs. frozen Southern-style hash brown potatoes
2 8-oz. cans tomato sauce
1 6-oz. can tomato paste
1 c. water
1 t. salt
½ t. basil
¼ t. pepper
1 lb. process American cheese, thinly sliced

Brown meat; drain. Add green pepper and onion; cook until tender. Add remaining ingredients except cheese; mix well. Spoon half of meat and potato mixture into 13½ x 8¾-inch baking dish or two 1½-quart casserole dishes. Cover with half the cheese. Top with remaining meat and potato mixture. Cover dish with aluminum foil. Bake in preheated 350° oven 45 minutes. Uncover. Cut remaining cheese into decorative shapes; arrange in patchwork design on casserole. Let stand 5 minutes or until cheese shapes have melted.

12 servings
Can be frozen

SAUERBRATEN STEAK
Chill: 8 hours or overnight
Cook: 2½ hours

2½ c. water
1 c. wine vinegar
1 T. brown sugar
1 t. salt
6 whole cloves
6 peppercorns
2 bay leaves
2 medium onions, thinly sliced
⅓ c. vegetable oil
1 beef blade steak (2½ to 3 lbs.), cut 1½ inches thick
2 T. drippings or cooking fat
¾ c. water
½ c. raisins
1 T. brown sugar
⅔ c. crumbled gingersnaps

Combine 2½ cups water, vinegar, 1 tablespoon brown sugar, salt, cloves, peppercorns and bay leaves in saucepan; bring to boil. Pour over sliced onions; cool. Stir in oil. Pour marinade over steak; refrigerate 8 to 10 hours or overnight, turning at least once. Remove steak from marinade to absorbent paper; pat dry. Heat drippings to 350°. Brown meat. Pour off drippings. Strain marinade; add 1 cup to steak, reserving remainder. Cover; cook 2 hours or until steak is tender. Remove steak to hot platter and pour off liquid. Add 1½ cups reserved marinade, ¾ cup water, raisins and 1 tablespoon brown sugar to frying pan. Bring to boil. Add crumbled gingersnaps; stir to thicken. Serve gravy with steak.

4 to 6 servings
Can be frozen

CHILI BEEF-SPANISH RICE RING
Cook & Serve: 3 hours

¼ c. flour
1 t. salt
1 t. chili powder
2 lbs. boneless beef, cut in 1-inch squares
3 T. shortening
¾ c. water
¼ c. dry red wine
1½ T. butter or margarine
1 small onion, chopped
¼ green pepper, chopped
½ t. chili powder
¼ t. salt
1 c. water
1 c. tomato juice
1⅔ c. instant rice
1 10-oz. pkg. frozen peas

Combine flour, 1 teaspoon salt and 1 teaspoon chili powder. Dip beef cubes in seasoned flour. Heat shortening; add beef and brown. Pour off drippings. Add ¾ cup water and wine. Cover; cook over low heat 2½ hours. After beef has cooked 2 hours prepare rice ring. Melt butter; sauté onion and green pepper. Add ½ teaspoon chili powder, ¼ teaspoon salt, 1 cup water and tomato juice. Bring to boil. Add rice. Cover; remove from heat. Let stand 5 to 7 minutes. Cook peas according to package directions. Drain and add peas to cooked rice; mix lightly. Pack peas and rice mixture into well-greased 1¼-quart ring mold. Let stand 2 minutes. Unmold onto heated platter. Fill ring with chili beef cubes. If desired, thicken cooking liquid with flour for gravy.

6 to 8 servings
Can be frozen

MOCK LOBSTER
Prepare & Serve: 45 minutes

1½ qts. water
1½ t. salt
1½ t. whole peppercorns
1 small bay leaf
3 slices lemon
1 large stalk celery, cut in 2-inch pieces
2 slices onion
1 lb. haddock or cod, partially thawed
Melted butter
Paprika
Lemon Butter Sauce

Combine water, salt, peppercorns, bay leaf, lemon, celery and onion in 3-quart saucepan. Cover; bring to boil. Simmer 10 minutes. Cut haddock or cod into bite-size pieces. Place in water; simmer 8 to 10 minutes. Remove carefully from water and place on broiling pan. Brush with melted butter; broil 4 inches from heat for about 3 minutes. Sprinkle with paprika. Serve with Lemon Butter Sauce.

2 servings
Can be frozen

STUFFED BAKED BASS
Bake & Serve: 1¼ hours
MARINARA SAUCE

1 6-oz. can	1 t. sugar
tomato paste	¼ t. pepper
2 c. water	½ t. dillweed,
1 T. lemon juice	crushed
¾ t. salt	

Combine all ingredients in small saucepan. Bring to a boil before pouring over fish.

STUFFING

2 T. chopped onion
2 T. chopped celery
¼ c. butter, melted
2 T. minced parsley
2 c. bread cubes
½ t. salt
¼ t. pepper
Dash paprika
½ t. dill seed
1 egg
1 large bass, coho salmon or any large fish
¼ c. chopped parsley

Sauté onion and celery in butter until golden in color. Add 2 tablespoons parsley, bread cubes, salt, pepper, paprika, dill seed and egg; toss lightly to mix. Add more melted butter, milk or sauterne to make sure dressing is loose. Wash fish, pat dry and fill with stuffing. Skewer or sew edges together loosely. Place in greased, shallow baking pan. Pour Marinara Sauce over fish. Sprinkle ¼ cup parsley over top. Bake in 350° oven 50 to 60 minutes or until fish flakes easily with a fork.

Allow 2 to 3 servings per pound
Can be frozen

VARIATION: Cook Marinara Sauce on top of range for 30 minutes and use as a topping for fish sticks. Bake fish without topping of Marinara Sauce and serve with equal parts melted butter and sauterne.

Pictured Opposite
Italian Broiled Fillets, p. 36

LEMON-CLAM SPAGHETTI
Cook & Serve: 30 minutes

8 T. (½ c.) butter
3 T. olive oil
1 medium onion, minced
2 garlic cloves, minced
2 8-oz. cans minced clams, drained,
　reserving liquid
3 T. lemon juice
1 T. chopped parsley
1 T. grated lemon rind
¼ t. pepper
1 bay leaf
1 gallon water
2 T. salt
1 lb. spaghetti
½ c. grated Parmesan cheese
　Lemon wedges

Heat 3 tablespoons butter and oil in heavy medium-size saucepan. Sauté onion and garlic until golden brown. Add clam liquid, lemon juice, parsley, lemon rind, pepper and bay leaf; simmer until liquid is reduced to about 1 cup. Remove bay leaf. Stir in clams; heat thoroughly. Add remaining butter; stir to melt. Bring water and salt to boil, add spaghetti and cook until tender yet firm, about 8 to 10 minutes; drain. Pour sauce over spaghetti. Sprinkle with cheese; serve with lemon wedges.

6 to 8 servings
Can be frozen

NOTE: One lemon yields 3 tablespoons lemon juice. Heat lemon for more juice.

ITALIAN BROILED FILLETS
Broil & Serve: 20 minutes

1 lb. fish fillets, fresh or frozen
3 T. soft butter or margarine
1 T. lemon juice
¼ t. salt
　Dash white pepper
½ t. crushed dried mint leaves
½ t. oregano
　Paprika
　Parsley sprigs
　Lemon wedges
　Black olives

Arrange fish fillets on greased broiler pan. Blend butter or margarine with lemon juice, salt, pepper, mint and oregano. Spread over fish fillets. Broil in preheated broiler 3 inches from heat for 3 to 5 minutes or until fish flakes easily when tested with a fork. Sprinkle with paprika. Serve hot garnished with parsley, lemon wedges and black olives.

3 to 4 servings
Can be frozen

BROILED GOLDEN PUFF FILLETS
Cook & Serve: 30 minutes

1 lb. fish fillets, fresh or frozen (cod,
　flounder, haddock, ocean perch)
　Salt
　Pepper
2 T. melted butter
¼ c. tartar sauce
1 egg white, stiffly beaten

Thaw frozen fillets. Place skin side down in well-greased shallow baking pan. Season with salt and pepper; drizzle with butter. Using medium heat, broil about 4 inches from source of heat for 10 to 15 minutes or until fish flakes easily when tested with a fork. Gently fold tartar sauce into beaten egg white. About 2 minutes before fish is done, spread egg white mixture over fillets. Broil until topping is golden.

3 servings
Cannot be frozen

Broiled Golden Puff Fillets

TUNA ROLL-UP
Bake & Serve: 1 hour

DOUGH

1¾ c. plus 2 T. all-purpose flour
1 T. baking powder
1 t. salt
¼ c. shortening
¾ c. milk

Spoon flour (not sifted) into dry measuring cup. Level off and pour measured flour into mixing bowl. Add baking powder and salt; stir to blend. Cut in shortening with pastry blender until mixture resembles coarse meal. Add milk, stirring with a fork until all flour is moistened. Turn out onto lightly floured, cloth-covered board. Knead gently twenty times. Roll to 9 x 15-inch rectangle ¼ inch thick. Spread Filling over dough. Roll up as for jelly roll starting at wide end. Seal ends. Place on ungreased baking sheet. May be shaped in a crescent if desired. Bake in 425° oven to 25 to 30 minutes. Serve hot with your favorite sauce.

FILLING

2 6½-oz. cans tuna
¼ c. salad dressing
¼ c. chopped sweet pickle
1 4-oz. can sliced mushrooms, drained
1 t. instant minced onion
1 t. salt
Dash seasoned pepper

Drain tuna. Combine ingredients and blend well.

6 to 8 servings
Can be frozen

Pheasant is considered a regal dish. It may be served roasted, braised, fried or stewed. Young pheasants that have been well-fed have a layer of fat under the skin. These birds can be prepared in the same manner as young chicken. If the birds are older or have less meat they should be prepared like older fowl . . . use moist heat to braise or simmer them.

BEER BATTER FOR FISH
Prepare: 15 minutes

1 c. beer
1 c. flour
1 T. salt
1 t. baking powder
1 T. vegetable oil
2 eggs, slightly beaten

Pour beer into mixing bowl. Combine flour, salt and baking powder and sift into beer. Stir with a wire whisk to blend. Add oil and eggs: continue to stir until batter is light and frothy. Stir batter occasionally to keep it thoroughly mixed.

About 2½ cups
Can be frozen

NOTE: Use small fish or fillets for deep fat frying. If fillets are large cut them in serving portions. Pat fish dry; dip fish in batter. Fry in deep hot fat, 370°, about 5 to 8 minutes or until golden brown. Drain on absorbent paper. Allow about ⅓ to ½ pound for each person.

GAME

PHEASANT IN CREAM
Bake & Serve: 2½ hours

1 pheasant (2½ to 3 lbs.), quartered
1 10½-oz. can condensed cream of mushroom soup
½ c. dairy sour cream
1 4-oz. can sliced mushrooms, drained
¼ c. grated Parmesan cheese
¼ c. chopped onion

Place pheasant in single layer in 13 x 9 x 2-inch baking pan, skin side up. In medium bowl blend together soup, sour cream, mushrooms, cheese and onion; spread over pheasant. Bake in preheated 350°oven 1½ to 2 hours or until pheasant is tender. Baste occasionally with sauce.

4 servings
Can be frozen

ROAST VENISON WITH SOUR CREAM GRAVY

Marinate: Overnight
Roast & Serve: 3 hours

2½ c. dry red wine
½ c. apple cider
3 bay leaves
4 whole peppercorns
1 6-lb. venison roast
  Salt
¼ c. (½ stick) butter
1 c. reserved marinade, strained

In shallow dish combine wine and apple cider. Add bay leaves and peppercorns. Place venison in marinade; cover and chill overnight, turning occasionally. Place meat on rack in roasting pan, fat side up. Sprinkle with salt. Insert meat thermometer in center of thickest part of meat, not touching bone or resting in fat. Place in preheated 325° oven. Meanwhile, in 1-quart saucepan melt butter; add reserved marinade. Brush meat occasionally with marinade mixture. Roast to desired degree of doneness (about 25 minutes per pound for medium rare). Remove roast to warmed platter.

SOUR CREAM GRAVY

1½ T. all-purpose flour
½ t. salt
¾ c. drippings from roast
½ c. dry red wine
1 c. dairy sour cream

In 1½-quart saucepan combine flour and salt; gradually add drippings, stirring until smooth. Add wine. Stir over medium heat until thickened. Reduce heat to low, stir in sour cream and heat to serving temperature.

6 to 8 servings
Can be frozen

EGGS

COTTAGE CHEESE SCRAMBLED EGGS

Cook & Serve: 20 minutes

6 eggs
¼ c. cottage cheese
2 T. milk
1 T. chopped chives
½ t. salt
  Dash white pepper
2 T. butter

Beat eggs in medium size mixing bowl. Add cottage cheese, milk, chives, salt and pepper; beat until blended. Melt butter in skillet over low heat. Add eggs to butter; cook slowly, turning portions of cooked egg with a spatula as they begin to thicken. Do not stir; do not overcook. Remove from heat when done; serve immediately.

4 to 5 servings
Cannot be frozen

PUFFY OMELET

Cook & Serve: 45 minutes

½ t. salt
¼ c. water
4 eggs, separated
  Dash white pepper, or tabasco sauce
1 T. butter

Add salt and water to egg whites. Beat until stiff and shiny and whites leave peaks when beater is taken out. Add pepper to yolks; beat until thick and lemon colored. Fold yolks into egg whites. Heat butter in 10-inch ovenproof skillet until just hot enough to sizzle a drop of water. Pour in omelet mixture. Reduce heat. Level surface gently. Cook slowly until puffy and lightly browned on bottom, about 5 minutes. Lift omelet gently at edge to judge color. Place in preheated 325° oven. Bake until knife inserted in center comes out clean, 12 to 15 minutes. To serve: tear gently, using 2 forks, into pie-shaped pieces. Invert "wedges" on serving plate so browned bottom becomes the top. If you like, omelet may be folded in half.

VARIATIONS: Prepare puffy omelet and serve with sliced or diced fresh fruit. Or thicken canned fruit (cherries, peaches or pineapple) and serve hot over omelet.

Prepare favorite omelet and serve with jam, jelly, preserves or sweet sauce.

2 to 3 servings
Cannot be frozen

Good, Fast & easy prep

SLIM CHICKEN BAKE
Bake & Serve: 1 hour

- ✓ 2 broiler-fryer breast halves, skinned
- ¼ t. garlic salt
- ½ t. paprika
- ¼ c. lemon juice
- 1 t. soy sauce
- ½ t. basil, crushed
- 4 pimiento-stuffed olives, thinly sliced

Season chicken breast halves with garlic salt. Sprinkle with paprika. Place chicken in shallow baking dish, rib side up. Combine lemon juice, soy sauce and basil; pour over chicken. Bake uncovered in preheated 400° oven for 20 minutes. Turn chicken and baste with juices. Top with sliced olives; continue baking 20 minutes.

2 servings
Can be frozen

DENIM DUMPLING DINNER
Cook & Serve: 4 hours

- 2 3-lb. stewing or frying chickens
- 6 c. water
- 1 T. salt
- 1 medium onion, sliced
- 3 stalks celery, cut in ½-inch pieces
- 1 carrot, cut in ½-inch pieces
- 2 c. cold water
- ¾ c. flour
- 2 12-oz. pkgs. frozen shredded hash brown potatoes, thawed
- 1 c. shredded sharp cheddar cheese
- ⅔ c. all-purpose flour
- 2 t. salt
- ¼ t. pepper
- 2 eggs, slightly beaten
- Snipped parsley

Simmer chicken in water and salt until tender, about 2 to 3 hours. Remove chicken meat from bones, leaving in large pieces. Skim fat from broth; measure broth; add water to make 4 cups. Add onion, celery and carrot; cover and simmer until vegetables are tender, about 15 to 20 minutes. Gradually add cold water to flour, stirring until well blended. Slowly add water and flour mixture to hot vegetables, stirring constantly. Cook until mixture boils and thickens. Simmer 3 minutes, stirring constantly. Return chicken to mixture. Place half of mixture in each of two 13½ x 8¾-inch baking dishes. To make dumplings, place hash brown potatoes in bowl and separate with a fork; stir in cheese, flour, salt, pepper and eggs. Drop by tablespoonfuls onto chicken mixture. Cover dishes with aluminum foil; bake in preheated 350° oven 30 minutes. Sprinkle with snipped parsley.

12 servings
Can be frozen

Slim Chicken Bake

OVEN FRIED CHICKEN (MEDITERRANEAN STYLE)
Bake & Serve: 1½ hours

3 lbs. broiler-fryer chicken pieces
2 T. soft butter
2 T. olive oil
2 T. lemon juice
1 to 2 t. oregano
1 t. salt
  Pepper
  Small whole potatoes or cooked white rice

Brush chicken with butter. Beat together oil, lemon juice, oregano, salt and pepper. Brush chicken pieces. Arrange skin side down in single layer in jelly roll pan. Bake in pre-heated 400° oven about 1 hour, turning once after 30 minutes. Baste chicken with juices after 15 minutes. Arrange potatoes in baking pan about 30 minutes before end of baking time.

4 servings
Can be frozen

NOTE: Whole chicken may also be used. Rub entire chicken including cavity with marinade. Bake in 375° oven 1½ hours.

ROSY LOW-CALORIE CHICKEN
Bake & Serve: 1 hour

3 broiler-fryer chicken breast halves, skinned
½ t. onion salt
2 T. sherry
¾ c. tomato juice
½ green pepper, diced
½ t. soy sauce

Season chicken breasts with onion salt. Place in baking dish. Combine sherry, tomato juice, diced pepper and soy sauce; pour over chicken. Bake, uncovered, in preheated 400° oven 40 minutes. Baste occasionally with tomato juice mixture.

2 to 3 servings
Can be frozen

DIRECTIONS FOR ROASTING TURKEY

To Thaw: Place turkey in original bag on tray in refrigerator. Allow 2 days for 8- to 11-pound bird; 2 to 3 days for 11- to 14-pound bird; 3 to 4 days for 14- to 24-pound bird. Refreezing is not recommended.

To Prepare: Free legs and tail from tucked position; remove neck from body cavity and giblets from neck cavity. Rinse and drain turkey. If desired, stuff neck and body cavities lightly, allowing ¾ cup stuffing per pound weight of uncooked turkey. Return tail and legs to tucked position. Skewer neck skin to back. Insert meat thermometer into center of thigh, next to body but not touching bone. Place turkey, breast side up, on rack in shallow, open pan. Do not add water or cover. Use following time chart.

APPROXIMATE ROASTING TIME—UNCOVERED PAN

Weight as Purchased	325° Oven
8 to 12 lbs.	3½ to 4 hours
12 to 16 lbs.	4 to 4½ hours
16 to 20 lbs.	4½ to 5 hours
20 to 24 lbs.	5 to 6 hours

Brush skin with melted butter to prevent drying. Baste frequently during roasting unless using a pre-basted turkey. When light golden brown, shield breast and neck with lightweight aluminum foil to prevent overbrowning. During last hour of cooking check for doneness.

To Test for Doneness: Before removing from oven, check to be sure meat thermometer is in original position. Thigh temperature should be 180° to 185°. Protect fingers with paper. Press thigh and drumstick. Meat should feel soft. Prick skin at thigh. Juices should no longer be pink.

BASIC STUFFING
Prepare: 20 minutes

8 c. soft bread crumbs
½ c. butter or sausage drippings
1 large onion, grated
1½ t. salt
¼ t. pepper
　　Seasonings as suggested

Tear or grate bread. (If using crusts, cut into fine shreds.) Mix together crumbs and soft butter, onion, salt and pepper. Add desired seasonings. Toss together lightly.

NOTE: A 1-pound loaf of bread makes about 10 cups of bread crumbs.

PORK SAUSAGE STUFFING

½ lb. pork sausage
　　Basic Stuffing

Brown sausage over medium heat, breaking apart with fork. Use sausage drippings in Basic Stuffing. Add sausage to Basic Stuffing and mix well.

SAGE STUFFING

2¼ t. sage
　　Basic Stuffing

Add to Basic Stuffing; mix well.

SAVORY STUFFING

¾ t. thyme
¾ t. sweet marjoram
¾ t. sage
　　Basic Stuffing

Add seasonings to Basic Stuffing; mix well.

About 9 cups
Can be frozen

ROBUST COUNTRY CHICKEN
Cook & Serve: 1½ hours

¼ c. flour
1½ t. salt
¼ t. pepper
1 broiler-fryer chicken, cut in serving parts
¼ c. vegetable oil
½ c. chicken broth
2 T. chopped parsley (optional)
1 12-oz. can yellow corn, drained
1 16-oz. can butter beans
1 T. chopped pimiento
2 8-oz. cans tomato sauce with mushrooms
1 t. seasoned salt

Mix together flour, salt and pepper. Lightly coat chicken with flour mixture. Heat oil in large skillet; lightly brown chicken on all sides. Pour off excess fat. Add broth; cover and simmer 40 minutes. Add parsley, corn, butter beans, pimiento, tomato sauce and seasoned salt. Simmer 10 minutes or until chicken is tender.

4 servings
Can be frozen

CHICKEN WITH HERB SPAGHETTI
Cook & Serve: 1 hour

¼ lb. butter or margarine, melted
½ c. parsley sprigs
2 cloves garlic, halved
　　Salt
⅛ t. pepper
1 t. basil leaves
½ t. oregano leaves
2 T. vegetable oil
1 T. lemon juice
2 lbs. broiler-fryer chicken pieces
8 oz. spaghetti
3 qts. boiling water
　　Parsley sprigs

Place butter, parsley, garlic, ½ teaspoon salt, pepper, basil and oregano leaves in blender. Cover; blend at high speed a few seconds or until parsley is finely chopped. (If you do not use a blender; mince parsley and use a garlic press.) Set 3 tablespoons of herb mixture aside for chicken and use the rest to toss with spaghetti.

Using a fork, beat together oil and lemon juice. Brush chicken pieces with mixture. Sprinkle with salt and pepper. Broil about 8 inches from heat about 45 minutes or until crisp and golden brown. Turn chicken after 20 minutes of broiling. Brush each side of chicken with reserved herb mixture during last 4 minutes of broiling.

Prepare spaghetti about 15 minutes before chicken is done. Gradually add spaghetti and 1 tablespoon salt to rapidly boiling water so water continues to boil. Cook uncovered until tender, stirring occasionally. Drain. Place spaghetti onto hot serving dish; toss with prepared herb mixture. Place chicken around edge of platter; garnish with parsley sprigs.

4 to 6 servings
Can be frozen

Pictured opposite
Puffy Omelet, p. 39

AUNT DESSY'S MOUSSAKA (EGGPLANT GRECIAN STYLE)
Prepare & Serve: 1½ hours

2 medium eggplants
Salt
Flour
⅓ c. olive oil
1 lb. ground chuck
2 medium onions, chopped
1 c. water
1 8-oz. can tomato sauce
½ c. minced parsley
1 clove garlic, minced
1 t. salt
¼ t. pepper
4 T. bread crumbs
2 T. grated Parmesan cheese
Cream sauce

Peel eggplants (leave some of the skin on in strips). Cut lengthwise into ¼-inch thick slices. Sprinkle with salt; strain in colander 20 minutes. Rinse off salt and lightly squeeze slices to remove excess water. Dip in flour and place in large oiled shallow pan. Drizzle oil over top; broil about 5 minutes on each side or until golden brown. Brown meat and onions in large skillet. Add water, tomato sauce, parsley, garlic, salt and pepper. Simmer about 20 minutes. Remove from heat; stir in 2 tablespoons bread crumbs and cheese. Butter 9 x 13 x 2-inch pan; sprinkle with remaining bread crumbs. Place half the eggplant slices in pan; spread meat mixture on top. Cover with remaining eggplant. Pour Cream Sauce over all. Bake in preheated 350° oven about 45 minutes or until golden brown. Cool slightly before cutting into squares.

CREAM SAUCE

4 T. (½ stick) butter
2 c. cold milk
3 T. cornstarch
Dash salt
2 eggs

In medium saucepan stir butter, milk and cornstarch over low heat until thickened, about 15 minutes. Stir in salt. Remove from heat; cool slightly. Beat eggs well; blend into sauce.

6 servings
Can be frozen

Don't be afraid to experiment with foreign foods. Even the most exotic-looking dishes are often easy to prepare if you follow directions carefully—and they provide a nice change of pace.

LAMB SHANK RAGOUT
Cook & Serve: 2¼ hours

3 strips bacon, cut in 1-inch pieces
4 lamb shanks or 2 lbs. lamb, fat trimmed
2 t. salt
1 t. celery salt
½ t. pepper
2 carrots, sliced
1 stick celery, sliced
1 onion, chopped
3 T. flour
1 6-oz. can tomato paste
2 c. water
1 c. red wine or brown stock
1 bay leaf, crumbled
¼ t. dried mint or 1 T. chopped fresh mint
¼ t. cinnamon

Cook bacon in Dutch oven until fat is transparent. Remove bacon, add lamb and brown, using 325° heat. Remove lamb. Stir in salts, pepper, carrots, celery and chopped onion. Sauté until onion is golden brown. Remove all but 2 tablespoons fat. Add flour, stirring to blend well. Return bacon and shanks to pan. Stir in paste, water and wine; bring to boil. Add remaining seasonings; simmer 1¾ hours.

4 servings
Can be frozen

Lamb Shank Ragout

CHICKEN CORDON BLEU
Cook & Serve: 1½ hours

3 whole chicken breasts (about 2½ lbs.), split, skinned and boned
4 oz. Swiss cheese (3 slices), cut in half
4 oz. (3 slices) boiled ham, cut in half
½ c. flour
1 t. salt
  Dash white pepper
2 eggs, slightly beaten
1 c. fine bread crumbs
2 T. butter
1 T. oil
1 10½-oz. can condensed cream of chicken soup
¼ c. light cream

Flatten chicken breasts with flat side of knife to ½ inch thick. Top each with ½ slice cheese, then ham. Fold each piece in half. Secure with wooden picks. Season flour with salt and pepper. Dip pieces in seasoned flour, then into egg; roll in bread crumbs. Heat butter and oil in large skillet. Sauté about 6 minutes on each side. Mix together soup and cream. Add to chicken breasts. Cover; cook over low heat about 50 minutes or until tender. Stir occasionally.

6 servings
Can be frozen

BEEF BOURGUIGNON
Cook & Serve: 2½ hours

4 slices bacon
2 lbs. beef chuck or sirloin beef cubes, about 1 in.
2 10½-oz. cans condensed beef broth or 2½ c. Brown Stock
1 c. Burgundy or other dry red wine
2 cloves garlic, minced
1 t. salt
⅛ t. pepper
⅛ t. thyme
⅛ t. marjoram
10 small onions (about ½ lb.)
½ lb. sliced fresh mushrooms
⅓ c. water
¼ c. flour
  Cooked rice or noodles

In Dutch oven or ovenproof pan, cook bacon until crisp. Remove and crumble. Brown meat in drippings; pour off all fat. Add bacon, broth, wine, garlic, salt, pepper, thyme and marjoram. Cover; bake in 350° oven 1 hour and 15 minutes. Add vegetables; bake 1 hour longer or until meat and vegetables are tender. Gradually blend water into flour until smooth; slowly stir into sauce. Cook, stirring until thick. Serve over rice or noodles.

6 servings
Can be frozen

CHICKEN CACCIATORE
Prepare & Serve: 1½ hours

¼ c. olive oil
1 t. salt
⅛ t. pepper
3 lbs. broiler-fryer chicken pieces
1 clove garlic, minced
2 medium onions, chopped
12 medium mushrooms, sliced
1 small green pepper, cut in large cubes
½ c. sliced black olives
1 8-oz. can tomato sauce
½ c. dry white or red wine
1 c. hot chicken broth
1 t. basil
½ t. dried mint
½ t. oregano
1 small bay leaf
  Cooked noodles
  Freshly grated Romano cheese

Heat oil. Salt and pepper chicken. Brown on both sides. Remove chicken; sauté garlic and onions until golden brown. Add mushrooms, green pepper and olives; place chicken on top of vegetables. Pour mixture of tomato sauce, wine, broth and herbs or 2½ cups Italian sauce over chicken. Bake in 350° oven 1 hour or until tender.

4 servings
Can be frozen

NOTE: This is another excellent chicken dish in which veal can be substituted. Use veal steaks or chops and cook 1 hour or until tender.

CHOW MEIN FOR A CROWD
Cook & Serve: 1 hour

2½ to 3 lbs. pork, cut in thin 3-inch strips
6 beef bouillon cubes
6 c. water
½ c. soy sauce
3 c. (6 stalks) diagonally sliced celery
3 medium onions, chopped
¾ c. cornstarch
3 16-oz. cans Chinese vegetables, drained (reserve ¾ c. liquid)
½ lb. fresh mushrooms, sliced
1 t. sugar
2 T. molasses type brown gravy sauce
1 16-oz. pkg. chow mein noodles

Heat large heavy skillet to 350°; add meat. Brown, draining off fat during and after browning. Add bouillon cubes, water and soy sauce; heat to boiling, stirring occasionally. Reduce heat. Cover and simmer 20 minutes. Stir in celery and onions; cover and simmer 10 minutes. Blend cornstarch and reserved vegetable liquid. Gradually stir into meat mixture. Add mushrooms, Chinese vegetables, sugar and brown gravy sauce. Cook, stirring until mixture thickens and boils. Boil and stir one minute. Serve over chow mein noodles.

12 servings
Can be frozen

HAM-CHESTNUT BURGERS
Broil & Serve: 30 minutes

2 c. diced cooked ham
½ c. chopped water chestnuts
⅓ green pepper, chopped
1 large diced tart apple
1 T. minced onion
¼ c. mayonnaise
¼ c. dairy sour cream
1 t. dry mustard
2 t. soy sauce
½ t. salt
4 hamburger buns, split and buttered
Buttered bread crumbs

Combine all ingredients except buns and bread crumbs. Spoon mixture over bun halves, spreading to edge. Sprinkle with crumbs. Broil until golden brown. Serve immediately.

4 servings
Can be frozen

CHINESE MEATBALLS
Cook & Serve: 45 minutes

1 lb. lean ground pork
¼ c. chopped water chestnuts
1 green onion, sliced
1 T. soy sauce
1 egg, beaten
1 t. salt
½ c. fine dry bread crumbs
Vegetable oil

Using a fork, lightly mix together all ingredients except oil. Form into ¾-inch balls. Heat oil in large skillet to 350°. Add meatballs; cook until browned. Drain on absorbent paper.

SAUCE

¼ c. cider vinegar
1 20-oz. can pineapple chunks
¼ c. firmly packed brown sugar
½ c. beef broth
1½ t. soy sauce
1 t. ground ginger
2 T. cornstarch
¼ c. water

While meatballs are cooking, drain pineapple, reserving ½ cup syrup. Combine vinegar, pineapple syrup, brown sugar, beef broth, soy sauce and ginger in small saucepan. Cook over low heat until sugar dissolves. Mix cornstarch with water; stir into brown sugar mixture. Cook, stirring, until thick and clear, about 5 minutes. Add meatballs and pineapple; heat thoroughly. Spear a pineapple chunk and meatball on wooden pick and serve.

4 dozen
Can be frozen

SOY SIMPLE CHICKEN
Cook & Serve: 1¼ hours

2 broiler-fryer chickens, halved
¼ t. salt
Pepper
4 to 5 T. soy sauce
Cooked wild rice

Season chicken with salt and pepper. Cover each chicken half completely with soy sauce. Place in shallow baking pan; cover with foil. Bake in preheated 400° oven 45 minutes. Uncover; cook 10 additional minutes or until tender. Serve on a bed of wild rice.

4 servings
Can be frozen

PORK-NOODLE CASSEROLE
Prepare & Serve: 45 minutes

2 T. butter
2 green onions, cut in ½-inch pieces
1 green pepper, cut in ½-inch pieces
1 stalk celery, cut in ½-inch pieces
1 clove garlic, minced
2 c. chicken broth
¼ c. cornstarch
2 T. soy sauce
1 T. bead molasses
½ t. salt
  Dash white pepper
2 T. dry white wine
2 c. diced roast pork
1 16-oz. can fancy Chinese mixed
  vegetables, rinsed and drained
1 3-oz. can chow mein noodles

Melt butter in saucepan; add green onions, green pepper, celery and garlic. Stir just until heated through. Combine broth, cornstarch, soy sauce, bead molasses, salt and pepper. Cook over low heat until clear and thickened, about 5 minutes; blend in wine. Stir in vegetable mixture, pork and mixed vegetables. Spoon into 4 buttered individual casseroles; line edge with chow mein noodles. Bake in preheated 350° oven 20 minutes or until hot.

4 servings
Can be frozen

MOO SHU PORK
WITH CHINESE FLATBREAD
Cook & Serve: 2 hours

1 lb. lean boneless pork, cut in thin
  3-inch strips
¼ c. soy sauce
2 T. dry sherry
1 t. cornstarch
½ t. sugar
1 clove garlic, minced
½ t. ground ginger or 2 thin slices
  fresh ginger, minced
¼ c. vegetable oil
½ lb. fresh mushrooms, sliced
1½ c. finely shredded cabbage
1 8-oz. can bamboo shoots, rinsed,
  drained and cut in thin strips
4 onions, sliced
2 eggs, scrambled slightly dry
1 16-oz. can sliced bean sprouts,
  rinsed and drained
  Chinese Flatbread

Combine pork, soy sauce, sherry, cornstarch, sugar, garlic and ginger in small bowl. Pour oil into a large skillet over high heat. When oil is hot, add meat mixture and cook, stirring rapidly, until pork is lightly browned. Add mushrooms, cabbage, bamboo shoots and onions. Continue to stir-fry until cabbage has begun to wilt. Add scrambled eggs and bean sprouts. Stir-fry to heat through. Place in warm bowl. Serve with Chinese Flatbread.

CHINESE FLATBREAD

2½ c. all-purpose flour
½ t. salt
1 c. boiling water
  Vegetable oil

In large bowl, combine flour and salt. Add boiling water gradually, blending with fork until mixture forms granules the size of peas. With hands, shape mixture into ball; knead about 5 minutes, until dough becomes soft and smooth. Shape dough into a cylinder about 16 inches long; cut crosswise into 16 slices. Cover unused slices with a damp cloth to prevent drying.

Place 2 pieces of dough on lightly floured board; roll each into a 3-inch circle. Brush tops lightly but thoroughly with oil. Place one piece on top of the other, oiled sides together; roll them together into 8-inch circle, being careful not to allow dough to wrinkle. Place an ungreased skillet over medium heat; cook each side 2 or 3 minutes, until blistered with air pockets and pale brown. Remove to heated plate. With fingers, separate the 2 layers. Cover with foil to keep warm. Repeat until all flatbreads are made. Serve hot. Flatbreads may be made a day ahead, wrapped and refrigerated, then steamed just before serving. To steam, put 1 inch of water in a large kettle. Place flatbreads on pie tin; support tin above water with custard cups. Cover kettle; bring water to boil; reduce heat. Simmer 10 minutes. 16 flatbreads.

8 servings
Cannot be frozen

ORIENTAL BEEF STEAK STRIPS
Cook & Serve: 1¼ hours

- 2 lbs. beef round steak, cut 1 inch thick
- 2 T. vegetable oil or cooking fat
  Water
- ⅓ c. soy sauce
- 2 t. sugar
- ¼ t. pepper
- 1 clove garlic, minced
- 3 carrots, pared and cut in thin strips
- 2 green peppers, cut in 1-inch squares
- 8 green onions, cut in 1½-inch pieces
- ½ lb. mushrooms, halved
- 1 8-oz. can water chestnuts, halved
- 2 T. cornstarch
- ¼ c. water
  Cooked rice

Cut round steak in strips ⅛ inch thick or thinner and 3 to 4 inches long. Heat oil to 350°. Add meat and brown. Pour off drippings, measure and add water to make 1 cup. Combine with soy sauce, sugar, ¼ teaspoon pepper and garlic; add to meat. Cover; simmer 45 minutes. Add carrots, green peppers, onions, mushrooms and water chestnuts. Cover; cook 15 minutes longer. Combine cornstarch and water and use to thicken cooking liquid for gravy. Serve with cooked rice.

6 to 8 servings
Cannot be frozen

PORK CHOPS ORIENTAL
Cook & Serve: 1¼ hours

- ¼ c. butter
- 8 loin pork chops, ¾ inch thick
- 2 c. chicken broth
  Pan drippings
  Chicken broth
- 1 6-oz. pkg. frozen pea pods, thawed
- 3 green onions, cut in ½-inch pieces
- 1 c. sliced water chestnuts
- 2 stalks celery, cut in ½-inch pieces
- 1 c. sliced fresh mushrooms
- 1 red bell pepper, cut in ½-inch pieces, blanched
- 2 cloves garlic, crushed
- ¼ c. cornstarch
- 1 T. soy sauce
- 1 t. bead molasses
- ¼ c. dry white wine

Melt 2 tablespoons butter over medium heat (350°); brown chops. Add 2 cups chicken broth. Simmer, covered, 45 minutes or until tender. Remove chops from pan and keep warm. Combine pan drippings and broth to make 2 cups; set aside. Melt remaining butter in saucepan. Stir in pea pods, onions, water chestnuts, celery, mushrooms, pepper and garlic. Heat just until hot. Combine pan drippings, cornstarch, soy sauce and bead molasses. Cook over low heat until thickened and clear, about 5 minutes; add wine. Stir into vegetable mixture. Place chops on heated serving platter. Spoon on vegetables.

8 servings
Can be frozen

Pork Chops Oriental

Outdoor Grilling

TERIYAKI HAMBURGER STEAK
Grill & Serve: 30 minutes

2 lbs. ground chuck
1 t. salt
¼ t. pepper
2 T. chopped fresh parsley
   Bottled teriyaki sauce
   Green onions, sliced diagonally

Lightly mix together beef, salt, pepper, parsley and 2 tablespoons teriyaki sauce. Form mixture into oval shaped steak, about 1¼ inches thick. Grill 3 inches from hot coals for about 8 minutes on each side. Brush with additional teriyaki sauce; grill about 5 minutes longer on each side. Carefully remove steak from grill with two spatulas. Serve with sliced green onions.

8 servings
Can be frozen

GRILLED PARMESAN TOAST
Grill & Serve: 15 minutes

½ c. soft butter or margarine
¼ c. grated Parmesan cheese
2 T. chopped fresh parsley
1 loaf Italian bread

In small bowl, blend together butter, cheese and parsley. Cut bread vertically into 1½-inch slices. Split each slice in half, taking care not to cut all the way through bottom crust. Spread insides of each bread piece with Parmesan butter. Place bread pieces on grill; toast about 5 to 7 inches above medium heat about 5 minutes on each side or until golden brown.

8 servings
Can be frozen

Pictured opposite
Spanish Olive Steak, p. 52

Teriyaki Hamburger Steak
Grilled Parmesan Toast

STEAK WITH COUNTRY SAUCE
Marinate: 1 hour
Grill & Serve: 45 minutes

1 2-lb. piece flank steak
1 t. garlic salt
  Dash ground pepper
2 slices bacon, diced
1 medium onion, chopped
1 T. cider vinegar
½ c. concord grape jelly
½ c. catsup

Sprinkle meat on both sides with garlic salt and pepper. In skillet fry bacon until crisp; push to one side. Add onion; sauté until golden brown. Add remaining ingredients and simmer until jelly melts and mixture is smooth; stir occasionally. Pour over steak and marinate 1 hour, turning steak after 30 minutes. Drain steak. Grill or broil steak to desired degree of doneness, brushing with marinade several times during cooking. Heat remaining marinade and serve as a sauce over slices of meat. Remember to carve against the grain of meat.

5 to 6 servings
Can be frozen

GOLDEN GLAZED CHICKEN
Grill & Serve: 1¼ hours

1 broiler-fryer chicken, cut in parts or quarters
¼ c. (½ stick) butter
1½ c. syrup (drained from 1 30-oz. can spiced peaches)
2 T. vinegar
1 t. soy sauce
2 T. prepared mustard
2 T. grated onion
1 t. salt

Place chicken in 2-quart shallow dish. In small saucepan, melt butter; add peach syrup, vinegar, soy sauce, mustard, onion and salt. Bring to boil; pour over chicken. Marinate until fire is ready for grilling. Baste generously while cooking, turning chicken every 10 to 15 minutes. Cook about 1 hour for quarters, 45 minutes to an hour for parts, or until fork can be inserted with ease and the juices run clear. If you like, season with more salt and pepper after cooking.

4 servings
Can be frozen

CHICKEN "BEER" B-QUED
Chill overnight
Grill & Serve: 1¼ hours

2 broiler-fryers, halved
1 12-oz. bottle beer
1 t. salt
¼ t. seasoned pepper
2 T. lemon juice
  Generous dash tabasco sauce
½ t. orange extract
1 t. grated orange rind
1 T. brown sugar
1 T. dark molasses

Place chicken in deep pan. Mix together remaining ingredients; pour over chicken. Marinate several hours or overnight in refrigerator. Grill chicken over hot coals about 1 hour; brush frequently with marinade while grilling.

4 servings
Can be frozen

SPANISH OLIVE STEAK
Chill: Overnight
Prepare: 30 minutes

1 blade chuck steak, cut about 1½ inches thick (3 to 3½ lbs.)
½ c. sliced pimiento-stuffed olives
2 cloves garlic, sliced
⅓ c. lemon juice
3 T. olive or salad oil
  Instant meat tenderizer
1 2-oz. can anchovy fillets, drained (optional)

Place steak in large shallow dish; top with olives. Combine garlic, lemon juice and oil; pour over steak. Cover and chill overnight, turning steak once. Remove steak from marinade and use tenderizer as label directs. Grill about 4 inches from medium-hot coals 10 to 15 minutes per side, or until desired doneness. Meanwhile, marinate anchovies in remaining olive marinade. Place steak on heated platter. If desired, arrange anchovies in a pattern of squares on steak; place olive slices in each square. Slice across the grain and serve.

4 servings
Can be frozen

Desserts

FROSTY SPICE CAKE
Bake & Serve: 1 hour

½ c. shortening
1 c. sugar
2 eggs
2¼ c. sifted cake flour
½ t. baking soda
1 t. baking powder
½ t. salt
2 t. cinnamon
1 t. cloves
¼ t. nutmeg
   Dash allspice
1 c. dairy sour cream
   Frosty Icing
⅓ c. chopped walnuts

Cream shortening. Add sugar; cream until light and fluffy. Add eggs, one at a time, beating well after each. Sift together dry ingredients; add to creamed mixture alternately with sour cream. Pour into 2 greased 8-inch cake pans. Bake in preheated 375° oven 25 to 30 minutes. Cool; frost with Frosty Icing. Sprinkle with walnuts.

FROSTY ICING

1 c. sieved firmly packed light brown
   sugar
2 egg whites
3 T. cold water
½ t. vanilla

Mix together sugar, egg whites and water in top of double boiler. Place over boiling water, being careful that water in lower part does not touch upper pan. Beat constantly with rotary beater until frosting stands in a point, 4 to 5 minutes. Remove top pan from heat. Add vanilla; beat 1 minute longer.

8 servings
Can be frozen

GLAZED WILLIAMSBURG ✓ POUND CAKE
Mix & Bake: 2½ hours

1 lb. butter, softened
3 c. sugar
12 eggs, separated
4 c. all-purpose flour, sifted twice
   Cranberry Glaze

Cream together butter and sugar. Beat egg yolks until thick and lemon colored. Beat egg whites until stiff peaks form. Alternately add yolks, whites and flour to butter-sugar mixture. Beat until light and smooth. Pour into greased and floured 10-inch tube pan. Bake in preheated 325° oven about 1½ hours or until golden brown. Cool in pan 30 minutes before removing. Drizzle cooled Cranberry Glaze over cake. Decorate with whole cranberries, if you like.

CRANBERRY GLAZE

2 c. water
2 c. sugar
1 lb. (4 cups) cranberries

In saucepan, bring water and sugar to rapid boil. Cook 10 minutes. Add cranberries. Cook until cranberries pop, about 5 minutes. Remove cooked cranberries with slotted spoon to a small bowl (put aside to serve with turkey dinner). Continue to cook syrup until thickened, about 20 minutes. Cool.

10 servings
Can be frozen

CHOCOLATE DREAM CAKE
Bake & Serve: 1 hour

1¾ c. sifted cake flour
1½ c. sugar
1 t. baking soda
1 t. salt
½ c. sifted cocoa
½ c. (1 stick) soft butter
1 c. buttermilk
2 eggs
   Quick Fudge Frosting
½ c. chopped pistachio nuts

Combine cake flour, sugar, baking soda, salt and cocoa in mixer bowl. Add butter and ⅔ cup buttermilk; beat 2 minutes on low speed of mixer. Add eggs and remaining buttermilk; beat 2 minutes longer. Pour into greased 13 x 9 x 2-inch pan. Bake in preheated 350° oven about 30 minutes. Cool 10 minutes. Remove from pan; cool on cake rack. Frost with Quick Fudge Frosting; sprinkle with nuts.

QUICK FUDGE FROSTING

    4 c. sifted confectioners' sugar
    ½ c. sifted cocoa
    ¼ t. salt
    6 T. boiling water
    2 t. vanilla
    ⅓ c. soft butter

Mix together sugar, cocoa and salt. Add remaining ingredients. Blend; beat until smooth and thick. If frosting becomes too stiff for spreading, stir in a few drops hot water. Makes 2 cups frosting.

12 servings
Can be frozen

After serving a cake—if you want to keep the cut surface fresh—just cover it with a strip of waxed paper. Use wooden picks to hold the paper against the cut portion.

MELBA CREAM CAKE ROLL WITH RASPBERRY SAUCE

Mix & Bake: 1 hour
Freeze: 3 hours

    4 egg yolks
    ¼ c. sugar
    ¼ t. vanilla
    4 egg whites, room temperature
    ½ c. sugar
    ¾ c. sifted cake flour
    1 t. baking powder
    ¼ t. salt
      Confectioners' sugar
    2½ pts. peach ice cream, softened
      Raspberry Sauce

Line bottom of 15 x 10-inch jelly roll pan with waxed paper; butter and sprinkle with flour; set aside. In large mixing bowl beat egg yolks and sugar until well blended; add vanilla. Beat egg whites in small bowl until foamy. Slowly add ½ cup sugar and beat until soft peaks form. Fold yolks into whites. Transfer mixture into large bowl when necessary. Sift together flour, baking powder and salt; sprinkle 1 tablespoon at a time into egg mixture, folding in gently. Turn batter into prepared pan; cut through batter with knife to release air bubbles. Bake in preheated 375° oven 12 to 15 minutes or until done. Loosen cake from sides of pan; invert onto towel generously sprinkled with confectioners' sugar. Peel off paper; cool cake 2 minutes; roll from short side in towel; cool completely. Unroll; cover ¾ of cake with softened ice cream and reroll. Wrap tightly in foil; freeze. Serve slices of cake roll with warm Raspberry Sauce.

RASPBERRY SAUCE

    2 10-oz. pkgs. frozen raspberries
    2 T. cornstarch
    ½ t. rum flavoring
    1 t. lemon juice

Drain raspberries; reserve juice. In small saucepan combine cornstarch with juice. Cook, stirring constantly until thickened; reduce heat. Cook 5 minutes; add flavoring, lemon juice and berries. Heat to serving temperature. Makes about 2½ cups.

10 to 12 servings
Can be frozen

Melba Cream Cake Roll with Raspberry Sauce

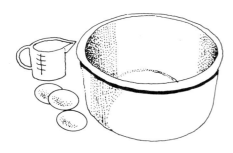

GRECIAN WALNUT CAKE
Bake & Serve: 2 hours

SYRUP

1 c. sugar	1 cinnamon stick
½ c. honey	1 T. brandy
1½ c. water	

Mix sugar, honey, water and cinnamon stick in small saucepan; boil gently 7 to 10 minutes. Cool; stir in brandy.

CAKE

- ¾ c. butter
- ¾ c. sugar
- 3 eggs
- 1 c. sifted all-purpose flour
- 1½ t. baking powder
- ¼ t. salt
- ½ t. cinnamon
- ¼ c. milk
- ½ t. grated orange rind
- 1 c. medium chopped walnuts
  Thin Confectioners' Icing
- 4 maraschino cherries, drained and quartered

Cream butter. Add sugar; cream again. Add eggs, one at a time, beating well after each. Sift flour, baking powder, salt and cinnamon; add to first mixture. Add milk and rind. Mix in nuts. Pour into buttered 8 x 8 x 2-inch pan. Bake in 350° oven 30 to 35 minutes. Cut in diamond shapes. While hot, pour Syrup over top. Cool 1 hour. Brush with Thin Confectioners' Icing. Decorate with quartered cherries.

THIN CONFECTIONERS' ICING

- 1 t. butter
- ½ c. confectioners' sugar, sifted
- 2 t. boiling water

Blend together all ingredients.

12 servings
Can be frozen

PLUM CRAZY CAKE
Mix & Bake: 1¼ hours

- 3 c. pitted and quartered plums (about 9)
- 1⅔ c. sugar
- 2 T. cornstarch
- 1 t. orange rind
- ½ c. orange juice
- ½ c. water
- ¼ c. (½ stick) butter
- 1 egg
- 2 c. sifted all-purpose flour
- 1 T. baking powder
- ¼ t. salt
- 1 c. milk
  Sweetened whipped cream

Arrange plums, skin side down, in 9-inch baking pan. In 1-quart saucepan combine 1 cup sugar and cornstarch; gradually add orange rind, juice and water. Cook over medium heat, stirring until thickened. Cook 2 additional minutes. Pour over plums. In mixing bowl cream butter; gradually add ⅔ cup sugar and beat until light and fluffy. Beat in egg. Sift together flour, baking powder and salt; add to creamed mixture alternately with milk, beginning and ending with dry ingredients. Carefully spoon mixture over top of plums; spread evenly to cover orange mixture. Bake in preheated 350° oven 45 minutes. Cool in pan on wire rack 5 minutes. Invert onto serving plate. Serve with whipped cream.

1 upside-down cake
Can be frozen

Plum Crazy Cake

VELVET FUDGE CAKE
Mix & Bake: 1 hour 10 minutes

    4 squares unsweetened chocolate
    ½ c. hot water
    ½ c. sugar
    2 c. sifted cake flour
    1 t. baking soda
    1 t. salt
    ½ c. vegetable shortening
    1¼ c. sugar
    3 eggs
    ¾ c. milk
    1 t. vanilla

Heat chocolate with hot water in top of double boiler or bowl. Cook, stirring constantly, over boiling water until chocolate is melted and mixture is thick. Add ½ cup sugar; cook and stir 2 more minutes. Cool.

Sift together flour, baking soda and salt. Cream shortening; gradually add 1¼ cups sugar. Cream together until light and fluffy. Add eggs one at a time, beating thoroughly after each. Add dry ingredients to creamed mixture alternately with milk, beating until smooth after each addition. Add chocolate mixture and vanilla, blending well.

Pour batter into 2 greased and floured 9-inch layer pans, 1½ inches deep. Bake in preheated 350° oven about 30 minutes; or bake in three 9-inch layers about 25 minutes or in 13 x 9 x 2-inch pan about 40 minutes.

12 servings
Can be frozen

NOTE: If butter or margarine is used instead of vegetable shortening, reduce milk to ⅔ cup.

PEANUT BUTTER-FUDGE CAKE
Bake & Serve: 1 hour

    1 c. (2 sticks) butter or margarine
    ¼ c. cocoa
    1 c. water
    ½ c. buttermilk
    2 eggs, well beaten
    2 c. sugar
    2 c. unsifted all-purpose flour
    1 t. baking soda
    1 t. vanilla

In medium saucepan combine butter, cocoa, water, buttermilk and eggs. Stir over low heat until mixture bubbles. In large bowl mix together sugar, flour and baking soda. Stir hot mixture into dry ingredients and beat until smooth. Stir in vanilla. Spread mixture evenly in greased and floured 9 x 13-inch baking pan. Bake in preheated 350° oven 25 minutes or until puffed and firm to the touch in the center.

TOPPING

    1½ c. creamy peanut butter
    1½ T. peanut oil

In small bowl mix peanut butter and oil until smooth. Cool cake in pan. Spread Topping evenly over cooled cake.

FROSTING

    ½ c. (1 stick) butter or margarine
    ¼ c. cocoa
    6 T. buttermilk
    1 1-lb. pkg. confectioners' sugar
    1 t. vanilla

In small saucepan, heat butter, cocoa and buttermilk until bubbly. Place sugar in large bowl. Beat in hot mixture. Beat until smooth. Stir in vanilla. Spread evenly over peanut topping. Cut into squares to serve.

1 9 x 13-inch cake
Can be frozen

BATTER-UP BROWNIES
Mix & Bake: 1 hour

    1 c. all-purpose flour
    ½ t. baking powder
    ½ t. salt
    ½ c. shortening
    1½ c. sugar
    3 eggs
    ½ c. peanut butter
    1 t. vanilla
    1 c. chopped peanuts
    1 6-oz. pkg. chocolate chips

Mix together flour, baking powder and salt. Melt shortening. Remove from heat and cool slightly. Add remaining ingredients in order listed. Mix thoroughly. Spread in well-greased 13 x 9 x 2-inch pan. Bake in preheated 350° oven 25 to 30 minutes. Cool in pan. Cut into squares.

About 2 dozen
Can be frozen

PEANUT CRUNCHIES
Mix, Shape & Bake: 1½ hours

1 c. (2 sticks) margarine
½ c. firmly packed brown sugar
2 egg yolks
1 t. vanilla
2 c. all-purpose flour
1 t. salt
2 egg whites, slightly beaten
2 c. chopped salted peanuts

Cream margarine and sugar. Beat in egg yolks and vanilla. Sift flour and salt together. Stir into sugar mixture. Shape dough into 1-inch balls. Dip in slightly beaten egg whites, roll in peanuts and place on ungreased baking sheet. Bake in preheated 375° oven 5 minutes. Remove from oven; press thumb gently into top of each cookie. Return to oven for 8 minutes. Cool. Fill with peanut-jelly filling.

FILLING

½ c. peanut butter
½ c. apple jelly
Mix together.

5 dozen
Can be frozen

BUTTERY PEANUT BRITTLE
Mix & Bake: 1¼ hours

2 c. granulated sugar
1 c. light corn syrup
½ c. water
1 c. (2 sticks) butter or margarine
2 c. raw or roasted peanuts
1 t. baking soda

Combine sugar, corn syrup and water in 3-quart saucepan. Cook and stir until sugar dissolves. When syrup boils, blend in butter. Stir frequently after mixture reaches the syrup stage (230°F). Add nuts when the temperature reaches soft-crack stage (280°F). Stir constantly till temperature reaches the hard-crack stage (305°F). Remove from heat. Quickly stir in baking soda, mixing thoroughly. Pour onto two baking sheets or two 15½ x 10½ x 1-inch pans. As the candy cools, stretch it thin by lifting and pulling from edges, using two forks. Loosen from pans as soon as possible; turn candy over. Break into pieces.

2½ pounds
Can be frozen

OLD-FASHIONED GERMAN COOKIES
Mix & Bake: 1½ hours

1 lb. salted red Spanish peanuts
3 egg whites, beaten stiff
3 T. flour
1 c. sugar

Grind peanuts in food chopper. Add stiffly beaten egg whites, flour and sugar; stir to mix well. Drop by teaspoonfuls onto greased and floured baking sheets. Bake in preheated 300° oven 15 minutes. Let cool before storing in cardboard boxes, where they will keep indefinitely (do not store in canisters or cookie jar).

5 dozen
Can be frozen

PEANUT BRITTLE COOKIES
Mix & Bake: 45 minutes

1 c. all-purpose flour
¼ t. baking soda
½ t. cinnamon
½ c. (1 stick) butter
½ c. firmly packed brown sugar
1 t. vanilla
1 egg
1 c. salted peanuts, finely chopped

Sift flour, baking soda and cinnamon together. Cream butter, add brown sugar gradually and cream well. Blend in vanilla and 2 tablespoons beaten egg (reserve remaining egg). Add dry ingredients and ½ cup peanuts. Mix thoroughly. Spread or pat dough on greased 14 x 10-inch baking sheet. Brush with remaining egg and sprinkle with remaining peanuts. Bake in preheated 325° oven 20 minutes. Do not overbake. Cut or break into pieces while warm.

1 14 x 10-inch baking sheet
Can be frozen

Remember to store soft cookies in loosely covered containers or cookie jars . . . crisp cookies in tightly covered containers. Do not intermix flavors.

SALTED PEANUT COOKIES
Mix & Bake: 1 hour

1 c. (2 sticks) butter or margarine
1 c. granulated sugar
1 c. firmly packed dark brown sugar
2 eggs
1 t. vanilla
1½ c. sifted all-purpose flour
1 t. baking soda
3 c. rolled oats
1½ c. salted peanuts

Cream butter; slowly beat in sugars. Add unbeaten eggs and vanilla; beat until fluffy. Sift flour with baking soda, add oats and stir into first mixture. Stir in peanuts, mixing well. Drop rounded teaspoonfuls onto ungreased baking sheet. Bake in preheated 375° oven 12 minutes.

6 dozen
Can be frozen

MY FAVORITE CHEESECAKE
Bake & Serve: 2 hours, 10 minutes

CRUST

4 T. granulated sugar
2¼ c. crushed graham cracker crumbs
½ c. (¼ lb.) plus 2 T. butter

Mix together all ingredients; line 9-inch spring form pan. Chill in refrigerator.

FILLING

1½ lbs. cream cheese
1½ c. granulated sugar
4 eggs
3 t. vanilla

Cream together cheese and sugar about 7 minutes. Add eggs and vanilla; beat 20 minutes on low. Pour into crust-lined pan. Bake in preheated 300° oven 1 hour and 20 minutes or until knife comes out clean when inserted in center. Remove; cool 20 minutes.

TOPPING

¾ pt. sour cream
1 T. granulated sugar
3 t. vanilla

Mix together all ingredients. Spread Topping over cooled cake; bake additional 10 minutes.

12 to 14 servings
Cannot be frozen

LEMON VELVET
Prepare: 30 minutes
Freeze: 4 hours or overnight

2½ c. graham cracker crumbs
⅔ c. margarine, melted
2 8-oz. pkgs. cream cheese, softened
1 c. sugar
2 T. milk
2 T. grated lemon rind
1 c. chopped walnuts
2 c. whipping cream, whipped
Lemon slices
Graham cracker crumbs

Combine 2½ cups crumbs and margarine. Press onto bottom of 13 x 9-inch pan. In mixing bowl, combine cream cheese, sugar, milk and lemon rind; mix until smooth. Fold in nuts and whipped cream. Spread mixture over crust. Freeze. Cut into squares. Garnish with lemon slices and graham cracker crumbs.

16 to 20 servings
Can be frozen

TRIFLE
Prepare: 30 minutes
Chill: 4 hours or until set

1 13 x 9-inch yellow cake
2 env. (about 2 oz. ea.) dessert topping mix
2 18-oz. cans vanilla pudding
4 T. sweet sherry
1 c. strawberry jam
⅓ c. toasted slivered almonds or chopped macadamia nuts

Cut cake in half crosswise. Cut each half into eight ¾-inch strips. Cover the bottoms of two 9 x 9 x 2-inch baking pans with approximately ½ of the strips. Prepare dessert topping mix according to package directions. Fold in pudding and 2 tablespoons sherry. Spread ¼ cup jam on cake strips in each pan; sprinkle each with 1½ teaspoons sherry; top with ¼ of the pudding mixture. Repeat with remaining cake strips, jam, sherry and pudding mixture. Sprinkle tops with toasted almonds or chopped nuts. Chill about 4 hours or until set. Cut each trifle into twelve 3 x 2-inch pieces.

24 servings
Can be frozen

PEANUTTY PIE
Prepare: 30 minutes
Chill: About 4 hours

1½ c. creamy peanut butter
1½ c. graham cracker crumbs
2 T. butter, melted
1 3-oz. pkg. vanilla pudding and pie filling mix
2 c. milk
1 c. whipping cream
¼ c. sugar
Roasted salted peanuts (optional)

Combine ½ cup peanut butter, crumbs and butter with a fork until well mixed. Press into 9-inch pie pan; chill. Combine pudding mix with milk; heat to boiling. Remove from heat and blend in remaining 1 cup peanut butter. Chill. Whip cream until soft peaks form. Fold in sugar. Fold whipped cream into pudding mixture; pour into pie shell. Chill several hours or overnight. Garnish with roasted salted peanuts.

6 to 8 servings
Cannot be frozen

Peanutty Pie

AN AMERICAN FAVORITE
Bake & Serve: 1¼ hours

FILLING

6 c. peeled and sliced baking apples
½ c. sugar
2 T. flour
Dash nutmeg
½ t. cinnamon

Combine all ingredients. Set aside while making crust.

PIE CRUST

1½ c. sifted all-purpose flour
½ t. salt
½ c. shortening
5 T. cold water

Sift together flour and salt; cut in shortening with pastry blender. Add water, one tablespoon at a time. Mix into flour mixture with blender. Turn out onto lightly floured pastry cloth. Bring ends of pastry cloth together; hit against table to form pastry into a ball. Divide in half. Roll one half in circle to fit 9-inch pie pan. Place filling into pastry-lined pan. Using scissors, cut off overhanging edges of lower pastry so it is ½ inch from the rim of the pan. Roll out remaining dough for top crust, making it 2 inches larger than pie pan. Carefully place evenly on top of filling, leaving a 1-inch rim of pastry beyond the edge of pan. If necessary, trim off any extra pastry. Fold extra crust under edge of bottom crust; press together. Flute edges. Bake in preheated 425° oven 35 minutes.

6 to 8 servings
Can be frozen

BRANDIED FRUIT COMPOTE
Prepare: 20 minutes
Chill: 4 hours

⅔ c. sugar
¼ c. water
1 slice lemon
3 T. brandy
1 pt. red raspberries
2 fresh peaches, peeled and sliced
Whipped cream (optional)

Heat together sugar, water and lemon slice in small saucepan about 10 minutes to make a syrup. Add brandy; mix well. Pour syrup over raspberries and peaches. Cover; chill about 4 hours. Serve with whipped cream if you like.

4 servings
Cannot be frozen

ANGEL MOCHA
Prepare & Serve: 45 minutes

1 9-inch angel food cake
24 marshmallows
½ c. strong, hot coffee
1 c. whipping cream
2 T. chocolate syrup
  Chocolate curls

Cut cake crosswise into 4 layers. Melt marshmallows in coffee over low heat; stirring often. Chill until partially set. Whip ½ cup cream; fold into coffee mixture. Spread between cake layers. Whip remaining ½ cup cream; fold into chocolate syrup. Spread on top of cake. Decorate with chocolate curls.

8 servings
Cannot be frozen

NOTE: To split a cake or torte evenly: measure the height of the layers you want; place wooden picks all around the cake and slice using a serrated knife.

BAKED ALASKA
Shape: 15 minutes
Freeze overnight
Prepare & Serve: 1 hour

1 pt. chocolate ice cream
1 pt. vanilla ice cream
1 pt. strawberry ice cream
  Foil
½ c. sugar
1¼ c. egg whites (about 10)
1 9-inch layer cake (white or fudge)
¼ c. brandy

Soften ice creams slightly. Line 7-inch bowl with aluminum foil, allowing several inches to extend over edge. Press chocolate ice cream into bowl; add a layer each of vanilla and strawberry. Cover; freeze overnight.

Add sugar to egg whites; let stand ½ hour. Beat until stiff peaks are formed. Place cake on wooden board. Unmold ice cream onto cake. Cover completely with meringue, sealing well. Brown in preheated 450° oven 5 to 8 minutes. Heat brandy; ignite. Pour flaming brandy over Baked Alaska.

6 to 8 servings
Cannot be frozen

PARTY ICE CREAM BOMBE
Prepare: 30 minutes
Freeze: 3 hours

2 pts. vanilla ice cream, softened
½ c. frozen concentrated pineapple-orange juice, partially thawed
1 pt. pistachio nut ice cream, softened
1 pt. raspberry sherbet, softened
  Toasted coconut

Chill 7-cup mold in freezer. Quickly spread vanilla ice cream as evenly as possible with back of spoon or spatula on inside of mold to make a shell lining about 1 inch thick. Return to freezer to harden ice cream. Spread ½ cup cup concentrated pineapple-orange juice in thin layer over ice cream; freeze. Layer pistachio ice cream into mold; freeze. Spoon raspberry sherbet into center to fill mold; freeze. To unmold, dip mold into warm water; turn onto chilled plate. Garnish top and bottom with coconut. Return to freezer to harden.

10 to 12 servings
Can be frozen

Pictured opposite
Party Ice Cream Bombe

INDEX

Thank you to the following for their cooperation and use of their photos: Charcoal Briquet Institute, Durum Wheat Institute, Frozen Potato Products Institute, La Choy Foods, National Broiler Council, National Fisheries Institute, National Livestock & Meat Board, Spanish Green Olive Commission, Swift & Company, United Dairy Industry Association, Universal Foods Corporation, Wheat Flour Institute.